John Clare

SELECTED POEMS

Edited by JONATHAN BATE

ff

faber and faber

First published in 2003
by Farrar, Straus and Giroux LLC, New York
First published in the UK in 2004
by Faber and Faber Limited
3 Queen Square London WC1N 3AU

Printed in England by Bookmarque Ltd, Croydon

ISBN 0–571–22371–0

The editor thanks Jonathan Galassi for commissioning this book,
John Goodridge and Bob Heyes for comments on a draft typescript,
and the Leverhulme Trust for funding his research

Title page: engraving of William Hilton's portrait of Clare, published
as the frontispiece to *The Village Minstrel*

2 4 6 8 10 9 7 5 3 1

CONTENTS

POEMS WRITTEN AT NORTHBOROUGH

JOHN CLARE: A CHRONOLOGY

(Some dates prior to 1818 are conjectural and approximate.)

1793 John Clare born on 13 July in village of Helpston, Northampton-
shire, in eastern flatlands of England, near market town of Stamford;
son of Parker Clare, casual agricultural labourer, and his illiterate
wife Ann; twin sister, Bessey, dies in infancy.

1797 Birth of childhood sweetheart, Mary Joyce.

1798 Birth of only surviving sibling, Sophy (she lives to 1855).

1798–1805 Attends 'dame school' in village, then school in neighbour-
ing village of Glinton, where he meets Mary Joyce. In hard times,
taken out of school to work as thresher with his father.

1799 Birth of future wife, Martha (Patty) Turner.

1805–8 Casual labour: ploughboy, potboy in local inn, weeding, tend-
ing of horses, gardening at nearby great estate of Burghley House.

1806 Reads, then buys, James Thomson's poem *The Seasons*, which
inspires him to become a poet himself.

1808 Attempts to enlist in militia; works as nurseryman.

1809 Parliamentary Act passed for the enclosure of Helpston and
neighbouring parishes. Earliest dated poem, 'Helpstone', first of
many protests at changes in landscape wrought by enclosure.

1809–17 More casual agricultural labour, including work with enclo-
sure gangs and a further period of employment on Burghley estate.

1812 Joins militia for periodic training.

1818 Family in dire poverty, father disabled by rheumatism; Clare leaves
home to find work as a lime-burner in villages beyond Stamford.

Meets Patty Turner. In December meets Stamford bookseller Edward Drury.

1819 Plans made for publication of first book of poetry; editorial work undertaken by Drury and his cousin, London publisher John Taylor (whose firm had published Keats's *Endymion*).

1820 *Poems, Descriptive of Rural Life and Scenery* published in January by Taylor and Hessey of London and Drury of Stamford; favourable reviews; quickly sells out and is reprinted three times within a year. Clare gains patronage of rival local aristocrats (the Fitzwilliams of Milton Hall and the Marquess of Exeter at Burghley). Visits London, where a subscription is arranged on his behalf by Lord Radstock. Portrait painted by William Hilton. Begins long correspondence with Mrs Eliza Emmerson, a well-to-do friend of Radstock who has become a passionate admirer of Clare and his poetry. Marries Patty in March, and first child, Anna Maria, born in June.

1821 Writes autobiographical 'Sketches in the Life of John Clare'; Taylor takes over publication of the *London Magazine*; Clare apparently sees his childhood sweetheart Mary Joyce for the last time. Second verse collection, *The Village Minstrel, and Other Poems*, published in September, in two volumes, including long autobiographical title-poem in which Clare represents himself as 'Lubin'. Second child dies in infancy.

1821–26 Works on long satirical poem, *The Parish*.

1822 Second visit to London; socialises with *London Magazine* circle of authors including essayists Charles Lamb and William Hazlitt, 'opium-eater' Thomas De Quincey, and Revd Henry Cary (translator of Dante). Second daughter, Eliza Louisa, born in June.

1823–25 First severe episodes of depression. Hears that 'shoemaker poet' Robert Bloomfield, whose work he much admires, has died in poverty. Plans for a third collection of poetry, *The Shepherd's Calendar*, but this volume takes four years to come to fruition; individual poems published in *London Magazine* and elsewhere.

1824 Eldest son, Frederick, born in January; third visit to London, where medical assistance is provided by George Darling, Keats's doctor. Witnesses funeral of Lord Byron, with whom he will later obsessively identify himself.

1825–33 Many individual poems published in magazines and literary 'Annuals'.

1826 Son John born in June.

1827 *The Shepherd's Calendar; with Village Stories, and Other Poems* published in April, after many delays; text heavily edited by Taylor.

1828 Fourth and final visit to London; son William Parker born in April; visit to Boston, Lincolnshire, where Clare sees the sea for only time.

1829 Dispute with Taylor and Hessey over accounts and literary earnings.

1830 Daughter Sophy born in July.

1830–32 Long periods of severe depression; brief involvement in local political journalism.

1832 Proposals printed for publication by subscription of new book, a substantial selection of his poems to be entitled 'The Midsummer Cushion'. In April moves with family to Northborough, village a few miles north-east of Helpston; immediately writes poem ('The Flitting'/'On Leaving the Cottage of my Birth') on how he is missing his old home.

1833–37 Increasingly ill with depression; continues to feel alienated in Northborough.

1833 Son Charles born in January.

1835 *The Rural Muse*, a collection of poems selected by Clare himself and Eliza Emmerson from the unpublished 'Midsummer Cushion', published in July. Clare's mother, Ann, dies in December, aged seventy-eight.

1837 Severity of depression, hallucinations and aberrant—possibly violent—behaviour cause Clare to be certified insane and taken in

July to Dr Matthew Allen's private asylum at High Beach in Epping Forest, Essex, on northeast edge of London. Remains under Allen's care for four years; is allowed considerable freedom to walk in forest.

1838 Mary Joyce dies, unmarried, of burns sustained in an accident.

1841 Writes long poems in voice of Byron, 'Child Harold' and 'Don Juan'. In July, walks out of the asylum and follows Great York Road back to his home in Northborough, a distance of over eighty miles covered in four days. On his return, writes up his recollection of the journey and copies out Byronic poems, adding more material to 'Child Harold'. In December, is certified insane for a second time and committed to Northampton General Lunatic Asylum.

1842–50 Considerable freedom to walk in hospital grounds and into Northampton. Continues writing poems, which are transcribed and preserved by William Knight, asylum steward.

1843 Son Frederick dies of tuberculosis.

1844 Daughter Anna Maria dies of tuberculosis.

1846 Father, Parker, dies, aged eighty-one.

1847–49 Some poems, including stanzas 'I Am', published in local newspaper, the *Bedford Times*.

1850–59 Following Knight's departure from the asylum, very few poems are preserved; Clare's health declines.

1852 Son Charles dies of tuberculosis.

1860–63 A few final poems written; health declines—series of strokes, some signs of senile dementia.

1863 Daughter Sophy dies, probably of tuberculosis.

1864 John Clare dies of 'apoplexy' (stroke) on 20 May; his body taken by train to Helpston, where he is buried five days later; Patty lives on until 1871.

INTRODUCTION

Sometimes you know from the colour of the sky and a peculiarly charged quality in the atmosphere that it is about to snow. At first there are only a few flakes. They fall very slowly, drifting down and sideways, even upwards, carried on the currents of air. There is something magical about this moment: we anticipate the still beauty of the whiteout to come, while our memory restores that ache of joyful longing we felt as children—when is there going to be proper snow in which we can play? It isn't easy to evoke those flakes in humdrum prose. We need poets to crystallise their motion for us, as John Clare does in a single perfect line at the end of his sonnet 'Open Winter': 'And snow in scarce a feather's seen to fall'.

The poetry of John Clare astonishes. It is astonishing that a man who suffered so much, both physically and psychologically, should have written so much and so well. It is astonishing that his achievement has not gained the recognition that it deserves—he was briefly known as 'the English Burns', but he has never become a household name in the manner of his Scottish counterpart. And astonishment is the mood of many of his best poems. He is amazed by seemingly inconsequential discoveries. 'Well,' he begins 'The Pettichap's Nest', 'in my many walks I rarely found / A place less likely for a bird to form / Its nest.' Then at the end of the poem:

> —Stop, here's the bird—that woodman at the gap
> Hath frit it from the hedge—'tis olive green—

Well, I declare, it is the pettichap!
Not bigger than the wren and seldom seen:
I've often found their nests in chance's way
When I in pathless woods did idly roam,
But never did I dream until today
A spot like this would be her chosen home.

Clare makes us feel as if we are strolling (he would say 'soodling') through the fields beside him. Along a hedgerow, through a gap into the woods. In his landscape there is always work to be done: the poems are peopled by woodmen, shepherds and milkmaids, all toiling and sweating, unlike the decorative figures of classical pastoral. But Clare takes time to pause and notice tiny things, such as the pettichap (otherwise known as the willow warbler). He feels an affinity with this shy and plainly plumed bird. He knew from experience what it was like to be frightened ('frit') from a nestling covert. He was a poet and naturalist in labourer's clothes, easily mistaken for a trespassing poacher.

The New Yorker John Ashbery—a writer very much of the late twentieth-century, whose work is urban, urbane, difficult—might seem to take poetry as far away as imaginable from the early nineteenth-century rural simplicities of 'the Northamptonshire Peasant Poet'. Yet he considers himself bonded to Clare, as Clare is bonded to the pettichap:

Clare grabs hold of you—no, he doesn't grab hold of you, he is already there, talking to you before you've arrived on the scene, telling you about himself, about the things that are closest and dearest to him, and it would no more occur to him to do otherwise than it would occur to Whitman to stop singing you his song of himself. It is like that 'instant intimacy' for which we Americans are so notorious in foreign climes. Clare bears you no ill will and doesn't want to shock or pain you, but that isn't going to make him change his tale one whit; if you suddenly burst into tears, that will seem to him another natural phenomenon, like the rain or the squeal of a badger.

He is apt to show you his wounds and crack a joke in the same moment; he is above all an instrument of telling.

Clare's art was to tell it as it is. In this, he was far ahead of his time. Closer perhaps to the American modernist William Carlos Williams, quietly noting a red wheelbarrow glazed with rainwater beside the white chickens, than to the archetypal Romantic poet William Wordsworth ratcheting up his spiritual response to a towering mountain or thundering cataract. So much depends upon what you want from poetry. If you want to know what a nightingale's nest is like in its intricate particularity you should read Clare, whereas if you want your nightingale to be a symbol of the eternal beauty of the poet's song you should read Keats. John Clare and John Keats were born within a couple of years of each other and shared a publisher, John Taylor, who was also a generous friend to them both. The two young poets admired each other's work, but Clare thought that Keats wrote about nature like a townie ('he keeps up a constant allusion or illusion to the Grecian Mythology'), while Keats thought that in Clare 'the Description too much prevailed over the Sentiment'.

For Clare, though, description is sentiment. He expresses his feelings by describing his world—his cottage, his corner chair, his garden, the beloved local places whose names roll off his tongue as if they were living friends (Royce Wood, Langley Bush, Swordy Well). If you do not believe that 'Love and Memory' (the title of one of his poems) are projected into particular objects and places, which should accordingly be treasured, then Clare is probably not the poet for you.

When Clare describes a place, a bird, a flower or a rural custom, he will often list its features. He tends not to privilege one detail over another, just as in his political vision he refuses to privilege the landed over the poor or the human over the animal, the vegetable and the land itself. At first sight, Clare's enumerations can make his work seem flat, as if in answer to the fenny flatlands of the eastern England that he knew. But a more attentive reading reveals that there is usually a circular motion in his writing, an answering not to the flatness of the land but to the curvature of the sky as it reaches towards the horizon.

One summer's day when Clare was still a child he started off in the morning to gather rotten sticks from the wood, but—as he recalls in one of his fragments of autobiography—he 'had a feeling to wander about the fields'. The yellow furze of Emmonsales Heath stretched away into the distance. He had often gazed in that direction. Now his curiosity got the better of him and he set off to explore. 'I had imagined', he recollected, 'that the world's end was at the edge of the horizon and that a day's journey was able to find it.'

He thought that when he reached the brink of the world he would find a large pit. He would look down and see the secrets of the universe, just as when he gazed into a pool of water he could see the heavens. As he put it in a long poem called 'Birds Nesting', written many years later,

> To the worlds end I thought I'd go
> And o'er the brink just peep adown
> To see the mighty depths below.

'I eagerly wandered on and rambled among the furze the whole day', he remembered, 'till I got out of my knowledge when the very wild flowers and birds seemed to forget me and I imagined they were the inhabitants of new countries'. On the heath, the sun shone from a different angle and each minute revealed a new world, a new wonder.

He was so absorbed in the scene that before the morning seemed to be over, it was dusk. A white moth fluttered, while snail, frog and mouse went on their evening journeys as 'the hedge cricket whisper[ed] the hour of waking spirits'. Clare found the right track by chance, 'but when I got into my own fields I did not know them—every thing seemed so different'. Not even the church, 'peeping over the woods', could stabilise his sense of where he was. When he got home he found his parents in great distress, and half the village looking for him. That day a woodman had been killed by a falling tree and they feared that the boy had suffered the same fate.

Clare spent many of his happiest days wandering alone on Emmonsales Heath. He grew intimate with the flora and fauna of his village and its surrounding parishes. His sense of his own identity was bounded by the horizon of his locality. To leave his home parish was to go out of his knowledge. To return was unsettling: the known and loved place seemed different. In reality, the village was the same. It was Clare who was different. Once a native has gone away, he can never fully return.

John Clare was born in the village of Helpston, Northamptonshire, in 1793. His father was a casual agricultural labourer with very little schooling but a great love of songs and ballads (and beer); he himself worked as a ploughboy, a reaper, a thresher, and a pot-scourer in the kitchen of the inn next door to his family's cottage. But he also became a reader, discovering James Thomson's elegant landscape poem *The Seasons* around the age of thirteen. To read the seasons in a book was perhaps to begin to lose the ability to live at ease with the seasons of the working life of the farm. Alienation was compounded when Clare's first love, Mary Joyce, was taken from him; her memory haunted the rest of his days, like that of childhood itself.

In 1820, his *Poems Descriptive of Rural Life* were published, followed the next year by *The Village Minstrel, and Other Poems*. His publisher brought him to London, where he was celebrated as 'the peasant poet'. He enjoyed the company of the authors who dined with John Taylor—Samuel Taylor Coleridge and William Hazlitt among them—but he felt ill at ease in the city. Back home in Helpston in the middle years of the 1820s he endured periods of severe depression. His relationship with Taylor was strained by arguments over editorial intervention, royalty payments and the delays surrounding his third book, *The Shepherd's Calendar; with Village Stories, and Other Poems*, which was eventually published in 1827.

In 1832, Clare's patrons and friends persuaded him to leave Helpston and move to a better-appointed cottage, with its own garden and orchard, in the village of Northborough, some three and a half miles away. To us the distance seems small, but for Clare—the miniaturist, the inhabiter of locality—removal to Northborough meant exile from all that he knew and all in which he felt secure. He marked his departure with a poem that in manuscript he called 'The Flitting'. It was published in his fourth book, *The Rural Muse* (1835), in abbreviated form and with the title 'On Leaving the Cottage of my Birth' (the printed text of the poem was accompanied by an engraving of the Helpston cottage):

> I've left mine own old home of homes,
> Green fields and every pleasant place;
> The summer like a stranger comes,
> I pause and hardly know her face;
> I miss the hazel's happy green,
> The bluebell's quiet-hanging blooms ...
> I miss the heath, its yellow furze,
> Molehills and rabbit-tracks ...
> I sit me in my corner chair
> That seems to feel itself from home ...

Northborough would never feel like a true home. Clare's insecurities mounted up and his family found it increasingly hard to live with him. In 1837 he was admitted, by authority of his wife, to a private lunatic asylum at High Beach in Epping Forest on the north-east edge of London. While he was there his physical health improved, but he had periods of delusion. He was allowed considerable liberty to walk in the forest. In 1841, he escaped and walked home to Northampton-shire, a distance of some ninety miles. Shortly afterwards, he was again removed, this time to Northampton General Lunatic Asylum, where he lived and wrote for a further twenty-two and a half years until his death in 1864.

The inhabited spaces of his childhood had disappeared during the very period when he was becoming a man. In 1809, Parliament passed an 'Act for Inclosing Lands in the Parishes of Maxey ... and Helpstone, in the County of Northampton'. Under the old 'open field' system there had been a sense of the community sharing the ownership of the land and participating in the time-honoured rhythms and rituals of the rural year. With enclosure, the 'fence of ownership' closed down the landscape and imposed a strictly economic ethic on the relationship between the villagers and the land. The 'commons'—meaning both the 'commoners' (as opposed to the proprietors) and the common heathland—were under threat.

> Moors losing from the sight, far, smooth and blea,
> Where swopt the plover in its pleasure free,
> Are vanished now with commons wild and gay
> As poets' visions of life's early day ...
> Fence now meets fence in owners' little bounds
> Of field and meadow, large as garden grounds,
> In little parcels little minds to please
> With men and flocks imprisoned, ill at ease ...
> These paths are stopped—the rude philistine's thrall
> Is laid upon them and destroyed them all.
> Each little tyrant with his little sign
> Shows where man claims, earth glows no more divine.
> On paths to freedom and to childhood dear
> A board sticks up to notice 'no road here'
> And on the tree with ivy overhung
> The hated sign by vulgar taste is hung
> As though the very birds should learn to know
> When they go there they must no further go.
> Thus, with the poor, scared freedom bade good-bye
> And much they feel it in the smothered sigh,

And birds and trees and flowers without a name
All sighed when lawless law's enclosure came . . .

('The Moors')

Clare regards enclosure as an impediment to dwelling in the world. The 'littleness' it brings is not that of miniature, but of the mean and grasping mind that encloses for the sake of economic gain. The birds are presented as victims of such minds every bit as much as the poor. The sign of the property-owner blocks the road to the freedom of the common land and in so doing also changes the configuration of the poet's mental space, severing the memory's way back to childhood. Jean-Jacques Rousseau compared 'the state of nature' to two things: childhood and a relationship to the land that is anterior to the proprietorial. In Clare's world, these two states are simultaneously foreclosed by enclosure. Poetry is the only place of freedom that remains to him.

ii

John Clare wrote over three and a half thousand poems. Less than a quarter of his total output was published in his lifetime. Poetry was his addiction. He knew that he wrote too profusely and that he needed editing. This anthology continues the work that was begun by the original editor to whom Clare owed so much, John Taylor. The aim of the selection is to offer a sampling from the full range of Clare's poems, thus demonstrating the breadth of his achievement.

The arrangement is chronological, so as to give a sense of Clare's development. The first section consists of half a dozen early poems that he did not publish: the delicate observation of a plant, a cheerful recollection of childhood, a sonnet on his twin sister who died in infancy, a lyric of erotic pleasure, an aesthetic meditation inspired by a country walk, and a poem of 'dedication' to his lost childhood sweetheart Mary Joyce. His art of minute observation and his ear for local language are already apparent in these early works: the leaves of the fern are 'crimped', while the benumbed hands of the schoolboys in winter are 'clumpsing'.

Clare's debut volume, *Poems Descriptive of Rural Life and Scenery*, is represented first by part of its lead poem, 'Helpstone', a long elegy in the manner of Oliver Goldsmith's *The Deserted Village*, inspired by the enclosure of the parish. This is followed by a lyric on the question 'What is Life?' (much admired by early reviewers), a reflection on what it is to be a poet from a humble background, three sonnets (on characteristic themes—a flower, a stream, a gypsy camp), and two songs (one of which was addressed to his wife Patty, the other of which was set to music and sung at the Theatre Royal Drury Lane). 'Helpstone' is an old-fashioned poem. The regular beat of its rhyming couplets is deeply indebted to a long tradition of eighteenth-century descriptive verse. Much of its language is hackneyed—labour is 'bustling' and the woodman's axe 'cruel'—but every now and then there is a line that could only have been written by Clare, as when he remembers how in the time before enclosure's ditching, draining and damming, a little stream 'O'er pebbles dimpling sweet went whimpering on'. Two of Clare's favourite words were 'sweet' and 'joy': they are his shorthand for both the unenclosed landscape and the freedom of childhood. Poems are the place where he squirrels away the memory of lost sweetness.

The title-poem of his second book, *The Village Minstrel*, is a long autobiographical narrative in elegant stanzas written in the form pioneered by Edmund Spenser in the Elizabethan period (an interlocking rhyme scheme and an extended final line to each stanza). This selection includes some stanzas from it concerning childhood games, stories and field-walks, together with a bitter sequence on the tyranny of enclosure:

> There once were lanes in nature's freedom dropt,
> There once were paths that every valley wound—

> Enclosure came and every path was stopped;
> Each tyrant fixed his sign where paths were found,
> To hint a trespass now who crossed the ground.

Clare's London patron, Admiral Lord Radstock, was not pleased by the stanzas that begin thus. 'Radical slang,' he huffed.

Seven further poems from the *Village Minstrel* collection reveal its principal themes: places and landscapes around Helpston, home and childhood, the seasons, the bond between mood and nature. Although Clare frequently figures the unspoiled landscapes of his childhood as a garden of Eden, he is always acutely aware that there is a long history to the relationship between place and people. The timelessness suggested by the image of Eden is modified by an acute sense of the workings of time. 'Swordy Well', one of Clare's favourite places for botanising and butterfly-watching, had been a quarry since Roman times; 'Langley Bush', a bower into which he retreats, had long been a meeting-place for gypsies and for a kind of early parish council known as the 'Langley Court'. Clare's sense of two different kinds of time is nicely caught by the double title of 'The Last of March (written at Lolham Brigs)': at one level, this is a poem about the cycle of the seasons, the return of warmth and flood and blossom in springtime, but at another level it registers the linear march of history as symbolised by the unknown graves of the Roman labourers who raised the causeway known as Lolham Bridges over the flood-plain to the north of Helpston.

A volume of a mere three hundred pages cannot do justice to Clare's long poems. Throughout the 1820s he worked on what he called his 'Cottage Tales', leisured verse narratives of village life and love, often based on the local folk tradition. These do not submit well to selection, so this is the one major genre of his work that is omitted from this anthology. His satirical and overtly political verse is, however, represented by three sections of *The Parish*, a long poem to which he returned many times but which was not published until the twentieth century. It has many passages that effectively mingle invective with comedy, but the whole is ultimately less than the sum of its parts. The section on the parish 'overseer' seems to have been inspired by the way the poet's father was treated when forced on to poor relief. The very word 'parish' had a double meaning for Clare. It referred to his community and the communal activities (holiday customs, games, stories) that kept people going through rough weather and economic hardship. At the same time, to go 'on the parish' meant to receive poor relief, to lose the dignity of independence.

Clare was especially admired for his descriptive writing on rural life. This aspect of his work was most fully developed in his third book, *The Shepherd's Calendar*. The whole of 'January' is included in the anthology, together with several brief selections from the remainder of this cycle of poems on the months of the rural year. The particular quality of 'January' is its combination of the outdoor and the indoor Clare. First he makes us feel the cold of the winter weather; then he draws us into the fireside, regaling the reader through the long evening with spine-chilling stories and traditional fairy-tales. As in a Dutch 'genre' painting, cottage life is vividly realised through the careful placing of everyday objects.

The Shepherd's Calendar is not only a descriptive work. It is also a political one: the poetry is written in order to preserve the 'old customs' that were being destroyed by the march of economic 'progress'. Clare's greatest enclosure elegy, 'The Moors', grew out of *The Shepherd's Calendar* (in his notebook it was originally drafted at the end of 'October'), so it is included at this point in the anthology, though it was not published in his lifetime.

The best of Clare's nature poetry is to be found in the body of work that he assembled for a fourth book. He wanted to call the volume *The Midsummer Cushion*, an allusion to a local custom of gathering flowers in summertime, but was persuaded by his London friend Eliza Emmerson to settle on the more conventionally poetic title *The Rural*

Muse. The selections printed here are divided into two sections, *The Midsummer Cushion* for those that did not reach the published volume and *The Rural Muse* for those that did. It must, however, be understood that they really belong together. These are the works of Clare's maturity, his most profound and accomplished explorations of his major themes: places and seasons, birds and their nests, childhood and memory, the philosophy of nature poetry, loss and change (see especially the marvellously assured writing of 'The Fallen Elm'), sexual desire and desolation, his artistic heroes (such as Lord Byron, the Lincolnshire watercolourist Peter de Wint, and fellow labouring poet Robert Bloomfield), the intimate link between creativity and longing ('hopes unrealized are hopes in reality', as he wrote in an autobiographical prose fragment). If there is one single poem that comes to the essence of Clare—an equivalent of Wordsworth's *The Prelude*—it would be 'The Progress of Rhyme', intended for the *Midsummer Cushion* collection but unpublished until the twentieth century. If there is another single poem that epitomises his gift of memory and lightness of touch in both rhythm and imagery, it would be the long poem 'Childhood', also omitted from the published collection (though published in parts in 1831 in a local newspaper, the *Stamford Bee*). And if there is a group of works that best reveals his sense of the matching architecture of the natural world and the poet's mind, it would be the bird and birds' nest poems, represented here by the nightingale, yellowhammer, moorhen, pettichap, landrail and skylark.

Very few of the poems written during Clare's five years' residence in Northborough were published in his lifetime. His depression was growing ever more severe and his black moods were exacerbated by the raw, bare (his word is 'blea') quality of the fenland environment to which he had moved. His work at this time was characterised by a feeling of exposure, a tone of increasing alienation. This period is represented here by, among other poems, an angry and politically-charged lament spoken in the voice of a piece of enclosed land (Swordy Well) and a series of remarkable self-identifications with shy and vulnerable creatures such as the snipe (a long-beaked marshland bird), the pine marten (a reclusive tree-climber of cat-like appearance), the badger and the field-mouse. Technically, Clare's finest accomplishment during the Northborough years was his development of new and wholly original patterns and rhyme schemes within the sonnet form. He never got around to ordering his sonnets for publication, but it is clear from the manuscripts that some of them were to be considered as sequences: the badger is first introduced at the end of the second sonnet on the fox and then runs through a series of sonnets of his own, until he is hunted down and killed in a sonnet that is cut off after twelve lines instead of the customary fourteen. This foreshortening is dramatic and purposeful. It suggests the end of a narrative line that began when the badger took over from the hunted fox, so in this edition—for the first time—Clare's badger (often anthologised selectively) is printed as a 'Sonnet sequence on Fox and Badger'.

Given the unfinished state of Clare's Northborough work, editorial decisions of this kind are unavoidable, as is the occasional provision of editorial titles for individual poems. Thus the sonnet that begins 'I found a ball of grass among the hay' sails here under a flag of convenience: the editorial title 'Field-Mouse's Nest'. For Seamus Heaney, Clare's poking of this ball of grass ('And progged it as I passed and went away') stands for his work more generally. Heaney's lecture, 'John Clare's Prog', written for the bicentenary of the poet's birth, proceeds from a close reading of the sonnet to the general observation that

> The poems of Clare's that still make a catch in the breath and establish a positive bodily hold upon the reader are those in which the wheel of total recognition has been turned. At their most effective, Clare's pentameters engage not just the mechanical gears of a metre: at their most effective, they take hold also on the sprockets of our creatureliness. By which I mean only that on occasion a reader

simply cannot help responding with immediate recognition to the pell-mell succession of vividly accurate impressions. No one of these is extraordinary in itself, nor is the resulting poem in any way spectacular. What distinguishes it is an unspectacular joy and a love for the inexorable one-thing-after-anotherness of the world.

When the old mother mouse bolts from the nest, her young ones are hanging from her teats. She looks simultaneously 'odd' and 'grotesque'. Clare makes poetry out of elements that are not conventionally beautiful as well as those that are. 'Field-Mouse's Nest' ends not with a picturesque dimpling stream of the sort that pervades Clare's early works but with a stagnant rainwater pool in the cavity that remains where peat has been dug out. The text printed here retains 'sexpool', Clare's original word for a peat pond, because the modernisation 'cesspool' used by most editors carries very different connotations. 'Sexpool' is an example of Clare's precise dialect that demands to be respected, even if it requires explanation in a glossary. The inclusion of glossaries in Clare's first printed volumes—a convention followed here—was the price for the preservation of his local language.

Heaney's lovely words about Clare's joy in the natural world perhaps underestimate the sophistication of his art. Many of the poems are as steeped in the language of the poetic and the biblical traditions as they are in the microgeography of eastern England. Clare is also supremely aware that to prog a nest may be to destroy it. Again and again, the poems find him at one with the creatures in the fields, yet also conscious of himself as an intruder, an outsider. That is why he is at once the poet of dwelling and of alienation.

Whilst in Dr Matthew Allen's private asylum for the insane, which was located in a beautiful setting in Epping Forest, Clare wrote some surprisingly calm sonnets and then a complex long poem with the Byronic title 'Child Harold'. A mixture of stanzas and songs, 'Child Harold' is spoken in several different voices and preserved in a fragmented and disorganised state. Some brief samples are included here, principally from the songs, most of which invoke the figure of Mary Joyce as Clare's lost muse. His other Byronic impersonation, 'Don Juan', is included in its entirety. It reveals an utterly different voice from that of the nature lyrics: a Clare who is angry, satirical, comical, topical, misogynistic, crude but intensely alive, a Clare who is at one level playing the role of Lord Byron while at another deluding himself with the belief that he actually *is* Lord Byron. By chance, when he was on one of his visits to London, he had witnessed the funeral of the most famous writer and lover in all Europe and the affection of the common people for the lordly poet had made a profound impression on him.

Clare's account of his walk home after escaping from Dr Allen's asylum is also included in the anthology, although it is written in prose rather than poetry. It is an extraordinary piece of writing that brings us closer than anything else to his immediate experience. It is followed by some fragmentary writings, in verse and prose, from the brief period before he was certified insane for a second time and removed to the Northampton General Lunatic Asylum.

Most of the surviving poetry from Clare's twenty-three years in the latter institution belongs to the 1840s. We owe its preservation to the asylum steward William Knight, who befriended Clare and wrote down his poems. This anthology's small selection from the large body of Knight's transcriptions places a particular emphasis on the 'visionary' voice that was new to Clare in these late works. Some of his most justly celebrated lyrics belong here, including 'A Vision', 'An Invite to Eternity' and the two astonishing self-revelations entitled 'I Am'. Removed from his native environment, Clare finds a voice that is peculiarly other-worldly. The asylum poems speak of desolation yet they are written with extraordinary assurance and a profound confidence in the approach of eternity—either in the religious sense or in that of achieving immortality through art:

I loved but woman fell away
I hid me from her faded fame,
I snatched the sun's eternal ray
And wrote till earth was but a name.

In every language upon earth,
On every shore, o'er every sea,
I gave my name immortal birth
And kept my spirit with the free.

The last two poems in the anthology, a beautiful sonnet addressed to his son (and namesake) back home and a return to his favoured image of the bird's nest as a place of safety, were written long after Knight had departed from the asylum and only shortly before Clare's own death at the age of seventy.

iii

Partly because of his 'peasant' origin and partly due to the sheer speed of his writing, Clare's voluminous manuscripts have very little punctuation and are highly irregular in grammar, spelling and capitalization. The poems that appeared in print in his lifetime were regularized for the press by his editors and publishers, notably John Taylor. The effect of this procedure has become the single point of greatest controversy among modern Clare scholars. Is justice done to him by the presentation of his manuscripts in the raw, free from the shackles of prescriptive grammar? Or does the reproduction of their idiosyncrasies unintentionally perpetuate the image of him as a semi-illiterate primitive, an eternal child?

Clare indicated in a note to his publishers that he expected his editors to normalize his spelling ('I'm' for 'Im', 'used' for 'usd', etc.) and to introduce punctuation for the sake of clarity, but he did not want them to over-regularize his grammar or remove the regional dialect words that were so essential to his voice. Editors of Clare from his own time until the 1950s duly added punctuation and corrected spelling, but John Taylor and his successors also changed words, phrases and whole sequences. The process of *normalisation* thus became entangled with that of *alteration*. Furthermore, the poor quality of Clare's penmanship and the inadequacies of his writing instruments meant that errors and misreadings were frequently introduced into the text.

Partly for this reason, a reaction set in during the 1960s: first Clare's text had been 'tidied up' by his publishers Taylor and Hessey, then it was 'botched' by later editors, so the time was ripe to reproduce his works in a form absolutely true to what he wrote. Such were the guiding principles of the scholars Geoffrey Summerfield and Eric Robinson when they began transcribing the original manuscripts and publishing them word for word. If Clare did not punctuate, neither would Robinson and Summerfield; since his spelling was erratic, so would be that of their text. Eric Robinson was later joined by other editors—David Powell and P. M. S. Dawson—in the production of a complete text of Clare's three and a half thousand or so poems, published in nine volumes by Oxford University Press between 1984 and 2003, based rigorously on the original unpunctuated and erratically spelt manuscripts.

But, as I show in my biography of Clare, the poet positively wanted his friends and publishers to assist him in the preparation of his work for the press. The final wording of many lines was reached via a process of dialogue that is frequently recoverable from surviving correspondence. Clare was closely involved with the editing and publishing of his first two books. His relationship with Taylor only became strained with his third book, *The Shepherd's Calendar*. For his fourth book, *The Rural Muse*, he again worked in harmony with both Taylor and his admirer and fellow-poet Eliza Emmerson. Then in the Northampton Asylum he relied on William Knight for the transcription of his poems. Clare was glad to be given advice, but did not always take it. Sometimes he acknowledged that his work was improved by his editors, whilst sometimes he stood by his own first thoughts.

As Clare used his critical self-judgement, so the modern editor should use critical judgement and analytical bibliography to decide on the status of the variations between manuscripts and printed texts—to distinguish between errors based on misreading of Clare's hand or misinterpretation of his sense, alterations that go against his spirit, and improvements of which he approved or is likely to have approved. This anthology is accordingly the first substantial selection from Clare's entire oeuvre to be prepared according to the principles that the poet himself wished to be applied to his work: the errors and unapproved alterations of earlier editors are removed, but light punctuation is provided and spelling is regularized without diluting the dialect voice.

Punctuation is the most difficult aspect of the editorial process. Clare wrote with great fluidity: phrase leads to phrase and image to image, circling out like ripples on a pond when a stone is thrown into still water. Often a line makes equal sense whether placed in apposition to the one before or the one after. As a simple example, consider the line 'The milking cows' guest' in the late asylum poem 'To be Placed at the Back of his Portrait' (page 296). Who is the guest in the dairy? The wren that has gone before or the 'Bard o' the mossy shed' (i.e. Clare himself) who comes after? The text printed here is punctuated in such a way that the phrase refers back to the wren because on all other occasions in the poem the invocation 'Bard of the . . .' starts a new sentence without any grammatical antecedent, but it cannot be *proved* that this was Clare's intention. The advantage of an unpunctuated text is that readers can make up their own minds about such decisions; the disadvantage is the implication that both readings are equally right—it seems implausible that Clare could have been thinking of both the wren and the bard as the cows' guest (otherwise he would have written 'guests').

This anthology is aimed at readers who are not familiar with Clare. In the absence of punctuation, many such readers often struggle with his sense and so lose the immediate impression that is one of the keys to his art. Once the reader has become familiar with the tone of his voice and the flow of his lines, it should become possible to ignore the punctuation and to find the pauses for oneself. That is best achieved by reading the poems aloud. Punctuation is a ladder that we need in order to climb to Clare's level; once we have got there, we can throw it away.

Of Clare's four collections, the one where his relationship with his editor became most fraught—and where there are the most differences between his manuscripts and the printed text—was *The Shepherd's Calendar*. Since this is the most complicated and controversial case, completely unedited transcriptions of parts of the original manuscripts of two poems in the collection are included, in order to give readers the feel of 'raw' or 'unedited' Clare. Among the manuscript selections is a sequence originally intended for 'October', but omitted and subsequently worked up into the enclosure elegy 'The Moors': by comparing the manuscript draft (pages 83–85) and the edited text (pages 89–91), the reader will gain some sense of the scale of the editorial task and the provisional nature of decisions about punctuation–an especially contentious matter in this particular poem, which is a protest against what might be described as the 'punctuation' of the open moorland that was enacted by enclosure. Some examples of unpunctuated manuscript lyrics are also included in the selection of writings from the five-month period between Clare's escape from the High Beach lunatic asylum and his admission to the Northampton one.

Extracts from longer poems are indicated by '*from*'. Titles in square brackets are editorial, others are Clare's own. The editor and publishers are grateful to the Peterborough Museum and Art Gallery and the Northamptonshire Libraries and Information Service, and also the

New York Public Library (courtesy Carl H. Pforzheimer Collection of Shelley and his Circle—Astor, Lenox and Tilden Foundations), for permission to consult the original manuscripts, and to Microform Academic Publishers for permission to produce edited texts of poems from their comprehensive microfilm copies of the Northampton and Peterborough collections (Wakefield, 1974–80).

Though all poems are edited afresh from manuscript and/or early printed editions, the Oxford Clare has frequently been consulted, and gratitude is expressed to Professor Eric Robinson and his colleagues for the painstaking scholarship that has revealed the full range of Clare's poetic achievement for the first time.* For more details of the textual problems and an account of other editions of Clare, together with suggestions for literary critical reading, see the Appendix and Suggestions for Further Reading in my *John Clare: A Biography* (New York: Farrar, Straus and Giroux; London: Picador, 2003).

JONATHAN BATE

The Early Poems of John Clare, ed. Eric Robinson and David Powell, 2 vols. (Oxford: Clarendon Press, 1989); John Clare, *Poems of the Middle Period*, ed. Eric Robinson, David Powell and P. M. S. Dawson, 5 vols. (Oxford: Clarendon Press, 1996–2003); *The Later Poems of John Clare*, ed. Eric Robinson and David Powell, 2 vols. (Oxford: Clarendon Press, 1984)—all copyright Eric Robinson.

Early Poems

To the Fox Fern

Haunter of woods, lone wilds and solitudes
Where none but feet of birds and things as wild
Doth print a foot track near, where summer's light
Buried in boughs forgets its glare and round thy crimpèd leaves
Feints in a quiet dimness fit for musings
And melancholy moods, with here and there
A golden thread of sunshine stealing through
The evening shadowy leaves that seem to creep
Like leisure in the shade.

Schoolboys in Winter

The schoolboys still their morning rambles take
To neighbouring village school with playing speed,
Loitering with pastimes' leisure till they quake,
Oft looking up the wild geese droves to heed,
Watching the letters which their journeys make,
Or plucking 'awes on which the fieldfares feed,
And hips and sloes—and on each shallow lake
Making glib slides where they like shadows go
Till some fresh pastimes in their minds awake
And off they start anew and hasty blow
Their numbed and clumpsing fingers till they glow,
Then races with their shadows wildly run
That stride, huge giants, o'er the shining snow
In the pale splendour of the winter sun.

To an Infant Sister in Heaven

Bessey—I call thee by that earthly name
That but a little while belonged to thee—
Thou left me growing up to sin and shame
And kept thy innocence untained and free
To meet the refuge of a heaven above
Where life's bud opens in eternity.
Bessey, when memory turns thy lot to see,
A brother's bosom yearns thy bliss to prove
And sighs o'er wishes that was not to be.
Ah had we gone together, had I been
Strange with the world as thou thy mother's love,
What years of sorrow I had never seen.
Fullness of joy that leaves no hearts to bleed
Had then with thine been purchased cheap indeed.

A Moment's Rapture While Bearing
the Lovely Weight of A. S—r—s

Unequalled raptures, happiest happiness,
For sure no raptures can compare with thee
Now lovely Anna in her Sunday dress
In softest pressure sits upon my knee—
For O to see the snowy bosom heave
And feel those robes to me so softly cleave,
Robes which half show what modesty conceals,
While round her slender waist I fling my arms
And while her eye what's wanting yet reveals,
To me appears such (more than heavenly) charms
That might I wish—and could I be so blest
To have it granted—O I'd wish to be
For ever of this matchless maid possessed
To bear her weight through all eternity.

A Ramble

How sweet and dear
To Taste's warm bosom and to health's flushed cheek
Morn's flushing face peeps out her first fond smile,
Crimsoning the east in many-tinted hue
The horizon round, as edged with brooding mist,
Penc'ling its seeming circle round so uniform
In tinge of faintly blue—how lovely then
The streak which matchless nature, skirting sweet,
Flushes the edges of the arching sky
And melting draws the hangings of the morn.
O who that lives as free to mark the charms
Of nature's earliest dress, far from the smoke
And cheerless bustle of the city's strife,
To breathe the cool sweet air, mark the blue sky
And all the nameless beauties limning morn
So beautifully touches, who when free
By drowsy slumbers e'er would be detained,
Snoring supinely o'er their idle dreams,
Would lie to lose a charm so charming now
As is the early morn—come now, we'll start,
Arise my dog and shake thy curdled coat
And bark thy friendly symptoms by my side,
Tracing the dewy plains we'll muse along.
Behind us left our nookèd track wild wound

From bush to bush as rambling on we tread,
Peeping on dew-gilt branch, moist grassy tuft
And nature's every trifle e'er so mean—
Her every trifle pleases much mine eye—
So on we hie to witness what she wears:
How beautiful e'en seems
This simple twig that steals it from the hedge
And wavering dipples down to taste the stream.
I cannot think it how the reason is
That every trifle nature's bosom wears
Should seem so lovely and appear so sweet
And charm so much my soul while heedless passenger
Soodles me by, an animated post,
And ne'er so much as turns his head to look
But stalks along as though his eyes were blinded
And as if the witching face of nature
Held but now a dark unmeaning blank.
   O Taste, thou charm
That so endears and nature makes so lovely,
Nameless enthusiastic ardour thine,
That 'wildered 'witching rapture 'quisitive,
Stooping bent, genius o'er each object—thine
That longing pausing wishing that cannot pass
Uncomprehended things without a sigh
For wisdom to unseal the hidden cause—
That 'ankering gaze is thine that fainly would
Turn the blue blinders of the heavens aside
To see what gods are doing.

Dedication to Mary

O Mary, thou that once made all
What youthful dreams could pleasure call,
That once did love to walk with me
And own thy taste for scenery,
That sat for hours by wood and brook
And stopped thy curious flowers to look
Where all that met thy artless gaze
Enjoyed thy smiles and won thy praise,
O thou that did sincerely love
The cuckoo's voice and cooing dove,
And stood in raptures oft to hear
The blackbird's music wild and clear,
That chased sleep from thy lovely eyes
To see the morning lark arise,
And made thy evening rambles long
To list the cricket's chittering song,
Thou that on sabbath noons sought bowers
To read away the sultry hours
Where roses hung the cool to share
With thee a blossom full as fair
Oft withering from noon's scorching look
And fluttering dropping on thy book
Whispering morals as they fell:
'What thou ere this hath proved too well,

Picturing stories sad and true
Beneath thy bright eyes beaming blue,
How youth and beauty fades and dies,
The sweetest has the least to prize,
How blissful pleasures fade away
That have the shortest time to stay,
As suns that blest thy eyes and mine
Are but allowed a day to shine
And fairest days without a cloud
A gloomy evening waits to shroud.'
So spoke the fading dropping flowers
That perished in thy musing hours,
I know not whether thou descried
But I could hear them by thy side.
But thy warm heart though easy wrung
Would not be melancholy long:
If such was felt, the cheering day
Would quickly chase their glooms away,
For thou sought fancies sweet to look
In every hour and every nook,
To thee earth swarmed with lovely things—
The butterfly with spangled wings
And dragonfly and humble bee
Hummed dreams of paradise to thee.
And O thou fairest, dearest still,
If nature's wild mysterious skill
Beams that same rapture in thine eye
And left a love that cannot die,
If that fond taste was born to last
Nor vanished with the summers past,
If seasons as they used to be
Still meet a favoured smile with thee,

Then thou accept for memory's sake
All I can give or thou canst take,
A parted record known to thee
Of what has been, no more to be:
The pleasant past, the future sorrow,
The blest today and sad tomorrow—
Descriptions wild of summer walks
By hedges, lanes and trackless balks,
And many an old familiar scene
Where thou hast oft my partner been,
Where thou, enrapt in wild delight,
Hast lingered morning noon and night,
And where to fancy's raptured thrill
Thy lovely memory lingers still,
Thy flowers still bloom and look the while
As though they witnessed Mary's smile.
The birds still sing thy favoured lays
As though they sung for Mary's praise,
And bees hum glad and fearless by
As though their tender friend was nigh.
O if with thee these raptures live,
Accept the trifle which I give—
Though lost to pleasures witnessed then,
Though parted ne'er to meet again,
My aching heart is surely free
To dedicate its thoughts to thee—
Then thou accept and if a smile
Lights on the page thou reads the while,
If aught bespeak those banished hours
Of beauty in thy favoured flowers
Or scenes recall of happy days,
That claims as wont thy ready praise

Though I so long have lost the claim
To joys which wear thy gentle name,
Though thy sweet face so long unseen
Seems type of charms that ne'er hath been,
Thy voice so long in silence bound
To me that I forget the sound,
And though thy presence warms my theme
Like beauty floating in a dream,
Yet I will think that such may be,
Though buried secrets all to me,
And if it be as hopes portray
Then will thy smiles like dews of heaven
Cheer my lone walks, my toils repay
And all I ask be given.

from
Poems,
Descriptive of Rural Life
and Scenery
(1820)

from Helpstone

Hail, humble Helpstone, where thy valleys spread
And thy mean village lifts its lowly head,
Unknown to grandeur and unknown to fame,
No minstrel boasting to advance thy name:
Unlettered spot, unheard in poets' song,
Where bustling labour drives the hours along,
Where dawning genius never met the day,
Where useless ignorance slumbers life away
Unknown nor heeded, where low genius tries
Above the vulgar and the vain to rise.
. . . .
Hail, scenes obscure, so near and dear to me,
The church, the brook, the cottage and the tree:
Still shall obscurity rehearse the song
And hum your beauties as I stroll along.
Dear native spot which length of time endears,
The sweet retreat of twenty lingering years,
And oh those years of infancy the scene,
Those dear delights where once they all have been,
Those golden days, long vanished from the plain,
Those sports, those pastimes, now beloved in vain,
When happy youth in pleasure's circle ran
Nor thought what pains awaited future man,

No other thought employing or employed
But how to add to happiness enjoyed:
Each morning, waked with hopes before unknown,
And eve, possessing, made each wish their own;
The day gone by left no pursuit undone,
Nor one vain wish save that it went too soon;
Each sport, each pastime, ready at their call,
As soon as wanted they possessed them all—
These joys all known in happy infancy,
And all I ever knew, were spent in thee.
And who but loves to view where these were past?
And who that views but loves them to the last,
Feels his heart warm to view his native place,
A fondness still those past delights to trace,
The vanished green to mourn, the spot to see
Where flourished many a bush and many a tree?
Where once the brook, for now the brook is gone,
O'er pebbles dimpling sweet went whimpering on,
Oft on whose oaken plank I've wondering stood
(That led a pathway o'er its gentle flood)
To see the beetles their wild mazes run
With jetty jackets glittering in the sun—
So apt and ready at their reels they seem,
So true the dance is figured on the stream,
Such justness, such correctness they impart,
They seem as ready as if taught by art.
In those past days, for then I loved the shade,
How oft I've sighed at alterations made:
To see the woodman's cruel axe employed,
A tree beheaded or a bush destroyed;
Nay e'en a post, old standard, or a stone
Mossed o'er by age and branded as her own

Would in my mind a strong attachment gain,
A fond desire that there they might remain;
And all old favourites fond taste approves,
Grieved me at heart to witness their removes.
. . . .
But now, alas, those scenes exist no more;
The pride of life with thee, like mine, is o'er,
Thy pleasing spots to which fond memory clings,
Sweet cooling shades and soft refreshing springs.
And though fate's pleased to lay their beauties by
In a dark corner of obscurity,
As fair and sweet they bloomed thy plains among,
As bloom those Edens by the poets sung,
Now all's laid waste by desolation's hand,
Whose cursed weapons level half the land.
Oh who could see my dear green willows fall,
What feeling heart but dropped a tear for all?
Accursed wealth, o'erbounding human laws,
Of every evil thou remainst the cause.
Victims of want, those wretches such as me,
Too truly lay their wretchedness to thee:
Thou art the bar that keeps from being fed
And thine our loss of labour and of bread;
Thou art the cause that levels every tree
And woods bow down to clear a way for thee.
. . . .
Oh happy Eden of those golden years
Which memory cherishes and use endears,
Thou dear belovèd spot, may it be thine
To add a comfort to my life's decline
When this vain world and I have nearly done
And time's drained glass has little left to run,

When all the hopes that charmed me once are o'er
To warm my soul in ecstasy no more,
By disappointments proved a foolish cheat,
Each ending bitter and beginning sweet,
When weary age the grave, a rescue, seeks
And prints its image on my wrinkled cheeks—
Those charms of youth that I again may see,
May it be mine to meet my end in thee
And, as reward for all my troubles past,
Find one hope true: to die at home at last.

What is Life?

And what is life? An hourglass on the run,
A mist retreating from the morning sun,
A busy bustling still repeated dream.
Its length? A minute's pause, a moment's thought.
And happiness? A bubble on the stream
That in the act of seizing shrinks to nought.

What are vain hopes? The puffing gale of morn
That of its charms divests the dewy lawn
And robs each flow'ret of its gem—and dies;
A cobweb hiding disappointment's thorn,
Which stings more keenly through the thin disguise.

And thou, O trouble? Nothing can suppose
(And sure the power of wisdom only knows)
What need requireth thee:
So free and liberal as thy bounty flows,
Some necessary cause must surely be.
But disappointments, pains and every woe
Devoted wretches feel,
The universal plagues of life below,
Are mysteries still 'neath fate's unbroken seal.

And what is death? Is still the cause unfound?
That dark mysterious name of horrid sound?

A long and lingering sleep the weary crave.
And peace? Where can its happiness abound?
Nowhere at all save heaven and the grave.

Then what is life? When stripped of its disguise,
A thing to be desired it cannot be,
Since everything that meets our foolish eyes
Gives proof sufficient of its vanity—
'Tis but a trial all must undergo,
To teach unthankful mortals how to prize
That happiness vain man's denied to know
Until he's called to claim it in the skies.

Dawnings of Genius

Genius, a pleasing rapture of the mind,
A kindling warmth to learning unconfined,
Glows in each breast, flutters in every vein,
From art's refinement to th' uncultured swain.
Hence is that warmth the lowly shepherd proves,
Pacing his native fields and willow groves;
Hence is that joy when every scene unfolds
Which taste endears and latest memory holds;
Hence is that sympathy his heart attends
When bush and tree companions seem and friends;
Hence is that fondness from his soul sincere
That makes his native place so doubly dear.
In those low paths which poverty surrounds,
The rough rude ploughman off his fallow grounds—
That necessary tool of wealth and pride—
While moiled and sweating by some pasture's side,
Will often stoop inquisitive to trace
The opening beauties of a daisy's face;
Oft will he witness with admiring eyes
The brook's sweet dimples o'er the pebbles rise,
And often, bent as o'er some magic spell,
Will pause and pick his shapèd stone and shell:
Raptures the while his inward powers inflame
And joys delight him which he cannot name,

Ideas picture pleasing views to mind,
For which his language can no utterance find;
Increasing beauties, fresh'ning on his sight,
Unfold new charms and witness more delight;
So while the present please, the past decay,
And in each other losing, melt away.
Thus pausing wild on all he saunters by,
He feels enraptured though he knows not why,
And hums and mutters o'er his joys in vain
And dwells on something which he can't explain.
The bursts of thought with which his soul's perplexed
Are bred one moment and are gone the next,
Yet still the heart will kindling sparks retain
And thoughts will rise and fancy strive again.
So have I marked the dying ember's light
When on the hearth it fainted from my sight
With glimmering glow oft redden up again
And sparks crack brightening into life, in vain,
Still lingering out its kindling hope to rise,
Till faint and fainting the last twinkle dies.
        Dim burns the soul and throbs the fluttering heart,
Its painful pleasing feelings to impart,
Till by successless sallies wearied quite,
The memory fails and fancy takes her flight.
The wick confined within its socket dies,
Borne down and smothered in a thousand sighs.

Patty

Ye swampy falls of pasture ground
And rushy spreading greens,
Ye rising swells in brambles bound
And freedom's 'wildered scenes,
I've trod ye oft and love ye dear
And kind was fate to let me,
On you I found my all, for here
'Twas first my Patty met me.

Flow on, thou gently plashing stream,
O'er weed-beds wild and rank,
Delighted I've enjoyed my dream
Upon thy mossy bank;
Bemoistening many a weedy stem,
I've watched thee wind so clearly,
And on thy bank I found the gem
That makes me love thee dearly.

Thou wilderness so rudely gay,
Oft as I seek thy plain,
Oft as I wend my steps away
And meet my joys again,
And brush the weaving branches by
Of briars and thorns so matty,
So oft reflection warms a sigh,
'Here first I met my Patty.'

The Primrose

Welcome, pale primrose, starting up between
Dead matted leaves of ash and oak that strew
The every lawn, the wood and spinney through,
Mid creeping moss and ivy's darker green;
How much thy presence beautifies the ground,
How sweet thy modest unaffected pride
Glows on the sunny bank and wood's warm side;
And where thy fairy flowers in groups are found,
The schoolboy roams enchantedly along,
Plucking the fairest with a rude delight,
While the meek shepherd stops his simple song
To gaze a moment on the pleasing sight,
O'erjoyed to see the flowers that truly bring
The welcome news of sweet returning spring.

The Gypsies' Evening Blaze

To me how wildly pleasing is that scene
Which doth present in evening's dusky hour
A group of gypsies centred on the green
In some warm nook where Boreas has no power,
Where sudden starts the quivering blaze behind
Short shrubby bushes nibbled by the sheep
That mostly on these shortsward pastures keep,
Now lost, now seen, now bending with the wind:
And now the swarthy sybil kneels reclined,
With proggling stick she still renews the blaze,
Forcing bright sparks to twinkle from the flaze.
When this I view, the all-attentive mind
Will oft exclaim (so strong the scene pervades)
'Grant me this life, thou spirit of the shades!'

The River Gwash

Where winding Gwash whirls round its wildest scene,
On this romantic bend I sit me down;
On that side view the meadow's smoothing green
Edged with the peeping hamlet's chequering brown,
Here the steep bank, as dropping headlong down,
While glides the stream a silver streak between,
As glide the shaded clouds along the sky,
Bright'ning and deep'ning, losing as they're seen,
In light and shade, to where old willows lean;
Thus their broad shadow runs the river by,
With tree and bush replete, a 'wildered scene,
And moss and ivy speckling on my eye.
O thus while musing wild, I'm doubly blest,
My woes unheeding and my heart at rest.

The Meeting

Here we meet, too soon to part,
Here to leave will raise a smart,
Here I'll press thee to my heart,
Where none have place above thee;
Here I vow to love thee well,
And could words unseal the spell,
Had but language strength to tell,
I'd say how much I love thee.

Here the rose that decks thy door,
Here the thorn that spreads thy bower,
Here the willow on the moor,
The birds at rest above thee:
Had they light of life to see,
Sense of soul like thee and me,
Soon might each a witness be
How dotingly I love thee.

By the night-sky's purple ether,
And by even's sweetest weather
That oft has blest us both together,
The moon that shines above thee
And shows thy beauteous cheek so blooming,
And by pale age's winter coming,
The charms and casualties of woman,
I will for ever love thee.

from
The Village Minstrel,
and Other Poems
(1821)

from The Village Minstrel

[*stanzas 3–16, on childhood*]

Young Lubin was a peasant from his birth;
His sire a hind born to the flail and plough,
To thump the corn out and to till the earth,
The coarsest chance which nature's laws allow—
To earn his living by a sweating brow.
Thus Lubin's early days did rugged roll,
Mixed with untimely toil; but e'en as now,
Ambitious prospects fired his little soul
And fancy soared and sung 'bove poverty's control.

Small joy to him were childhood's tempting tricks,
Which schoolboys look for in their vacant hours;
With other boys he little cared to mix;
Joy left him lonely in his hawthorn bowers,
As haply binding up his knots of flowers,
Or list'ning unseen birds to hear them sing;
Or gazing downward where the runnel pours
Through the mossed bridge in many a whirling ring,
How would he muse o'er all on pleasure's fairy wing.

The 'I spy', 'halloo', and the marble-ring,
And many a game that infancy employs,

The spinning-top whirled from the twitching string,
The boastful jump of strong exulting boys,
Their sports, their pastimes, all their pleasing toys
We leave unsung—though much such rural play
Would suit the theme—yet they're not Lubin's joys:
Truth breathes the song in Lubin's steps to stray
Through woods and fields and plains his solitary way,

And tell how vales and shades did please his sight,
And how the wind breathed music through each bough,
And how in rural charms he did delight—
To mark the shepherd's folds and swains at plough
And pasture specked with sheep and horse and cow,
With many a beauty that does intervene,
And steeple peeping o'er the wood's dark brow;
While young hope's fancy popped its smile between
And wished man's days to spend in some such peaceful scene.

Each opening season and each opening scene
On his wild view still teemed with fresh delight;
E'en winter's storms to him have welcome been
That brought him comfort in its long dark night
As joyful list'ning, while the fire burnt bright,
Some neighbouring labourer's superstitious tale,
How 'Jinny-burnt-arse' with her wisp alight
To drown a 'nighted traveller once did fail,
He knowing well the brook that whimpered down the vale.

And tales of fairy-land he loved to hear,
Those mites of human forms, like skimming bees,
That fly and flirt about but everywhere,
The mystic tribes of night's unnerving breeze

That through a lock-hole even creep with ease:
The freaks and stories of this elfin crew,
Ah, Lubin gloried in such things as these;
How they rewarded industry he knew,
And how the restless slut was pinchèd black and blue.

How ancient dames a fairy's anger feared,
From gossips' stories Lubin often heard:
How they but every night the hearth-stone cleared,
And 'gainst their visits all things neat prepared,
As fays naught more than cleanliness regard;
When in the morn they never failed to share
Or gold or silver as their meet reward,
Dropt in the water superstition's care
To make the charm succeed had cautious placèd there.

And thousands such the village keeps alive:
Beings that people superstitious earth,
That e'er in rural manners will survive
As long as wild rusticity has birth
To spread their wonders round the cottage-hearth.
On Lubin's mind these deeply were impressed;
Oft fear forbade to share his neighbour's mirth—
And long each tale by fancy newly dressed
Brought fairies in his dreams and broke his infant rest.

He had his dreads and fears, and scarce could pass
A churchyard's dreary mounds at silent night,
But footsteps trampled through the rustling grass
And ghosts 'hind grave-stones stood in sheets of white,
Dread monsters fancy moulded on his sight:
Soft would he step lest they his tread should hear

And creep and creep till past his wild affright;
Then on wind's wings would rally as it were,
So swift the wild retreat of childhood's fancied fear.

And when fear left him, on his corner-seat
Much would he chatter o'er each dreadful tale:
Tell how he heard the sound of 'proaching feet
And warriors jingling in their coats of mail,
And lumping knocks, as one would thump a flail,
Of spirits conjured in the charnel floor,
And many a mournful shriek and hapless wail
Where maids self-murdered their false loves deplore—
And from that time would vow to tramp on nights no more.

O who can speak his joys when spring's young morn
From wood and pasture opened on his view,
When tender green buds blush upon the thorn
And the first primrose dips its leaves in dew:
Each varied charm how joyed would he pursue,
Tempted to trace their beauties through the day;
Grey-girdled eve and morn of rosy hue
Have both beheld him on his lonely way,
Far, far remote from boys and their unpleasing play.

Sequestered nature was his heart's delight;
Him would she lead through wood and lonely plain,
Searching the pooty from the rushy dyke;
And while the thrush sang her long-silenced strain,
He thought it sweet and mocked it o'er again;
And while he plucked the primrose in its pride,
He pondered o'er its bloom 'tween joy and pain,
And a rude sonnet in its praise he tried,
Where nature's simple way the aid of art supplied.

The freshened landscapes round his routes unfurled,
The fine-tinged clouds above, the woods below,
Each met his eye a new-revealing world,
Delighting more as more he learned to know,
Each journey sweeter, musing to and fro.
Surrounded thus, not paradise more sweet,
Enthusiasm made his soul to glow;
His heart with wild sensations used to beat;
As nature seemly sang, his mutterings would repeat.

Upon a molehill oft he dropt him down,
To take a prospect of the circling scene,
Marking how much the cottage roof's-thatch brown
Did add its beauty to the budding green
Of sheltering trees it humbly peeped between—
The stone-rocked wagon with its rumbling sound,
The windmill's sweeping sails at distance seen,
And every form that crowds the circling round,
Where the sky stooping seems to kiss the meeting ground.

[*stanzas 90–97, on enclosure*]

But who can tell the anguish of his mind
When reformation's formidable foes
With civil wars 'gainst nature's peace combined,
And desolation struck her deadly blows
As curst improvement 'gan his fields inclose:
O greens and fields and trees, farewell, farewell!
His heart-wrung pains, his unavailing woes
No words can utter and no tongue can tell,
When ploughs destroyed the green, when groves of willows fell.

There once were springs when daisies' silver studs
Like sheets of snow on every pasture spread;
There once were summers when the crow-flower buds
Like golden sunbeams brightest lustre shed;
And trees grew once that sheltered Lubin's head;
There once were brooks sweet whimpering down the vale:
The brook's no more—kingcup and daisy fled,
Their last fallen tree the naked moors bewail
And scarce a bush is left to tell the mournful tale.

Yon shaggy tufts and many a rushy knot
Existing still in spite of spade and plough,
As seeming fond and loath to leave the spot,
Tell where was once the green—brown fallows now,
Where Lubin often turns a saddened brow,
Marks the stopped brook and mourns oppression's power,
And thinks how once he waded in each slough
To crop the yellow 'horse-blob's' early flower
Or catch the 'miller's-thumb' in summer's sultry hour.

There once were days, the woodman knows it well,
When shades e'en echoed with the singing thrush;
There once were hours, the ploughman's tale can tell,
When morning's beauty wore its earliest blush,
How woodlarks carolled from each stumpy bush;
Lubin himself has marked them soar and sing:
The thorns are gone, the woodlark's song is hush,
Spring more resembles winter now than spring,
The shades are banished all—the birds have took to wing.

There once were lanes in nature's freedom dropt,
There once were paths that every valley wound—

Enclosure came and every path was stopped;
Each tyrant fixed his sign where paths were found,
To hint a trespass now who crossed the ground:
Justice is made to speak as they command;
The high road now must be each stinted bound:
—Enclosure, thou'rt a curse upon the land
And tasteless was the wretch who thy existence planned.

O England, boasted land of liberty,
With strangers still thou mayst thy title own,
But thy poor slaves the alteration see,
With many a loss to them the truth is known:
Like emigrating bird thy freedom's flown,
While mongrel clowns, low as their rooting plough,
Disdain thy laws to put in force their own;
And every village owns its tyrants now,
And parish-slaves must live as parish-kings allow.

Ye fields, ye scenes so dear to Lubin's eye,
Ye meadow-blooms, ye pasture-flowers, farewell!
Ye banished trees, ye make me deeply sigh—
Enclosure came and all your glories fell:
E'en the old oak that crowned yon rifled dell,
Whose age had made it sacred to the view,
Not long was left his children's fate to tell;
Where ignorance and wealth their course pursue,
Each tree must tumble down—old 'Lea-close Oak,' adieu!

Lubin beheld it all and, deeply pained,
Along the palèd road would muse and sigh—
The only path that freedom's rights maintained—
The naked scenes drew pity from his eye,

Tears dropt to memory of delights gone by:
The haunts of freedom, cowherd's wattled bower
And shepherd's huts and trees that towered high
And spreading thorns that turned a summer shower,
All captives lost and past to sad oppression's power.

Song

Swamps of wild rush-beds and sloughs' squashy traces,
    Grounds of rough fallows with thistle and weed,
Flats and low valleys of kingcups and daisies,
    Sweetest of subjects are ye for my reed:
Ye commons left free in the rude rags of nature,
    Ye brown heaths beclothed in furze as ye be,
My wild eye in rapture adores every feature,
    Ye are dear as this heart in my bosom to me.

O native endearments, I would not forsake ye,
    I would not forsake ye for sweetest of scenes;
For sweetest of gardens that nature could make me,
    I would not forsake ye, dear valleys and greens:
Though nature ne'er dropt ye a cloud-resting mountain,
    Nor waterfalls tumble their music so free;
Had nature denied ye a bush, tree, or fountain,
    Ye still had been loved as an Eden by me.

And long, my dear valleys, long, long may ye flourish,
    Though rush-beds and thistles make most of your pride;
May showers never fail the green's daisies to nourish,
    Nor suns dry the fountain that rills by its side.
Your skies may be gloomy and misty your mornings,
    Your flat swampy valleys unwholesome may be;
Still, refuse of nature, without her adornings
    Ye are dear as this heart in my bosom to me.

To an Infant Daughter

Sweet gem of infant fairy-flowers,
Thy smiles on life's unclosing hours
Like sunbeams lost in summer showers,
      They wake my fears;
When reason knows its sweets and sours,
      They'll change to tears.

God help thee, little senseless thing,
Thou, daisy-like of early spring,
Of ambushed winter's hornet sting
      Hast yet to tell;
Thou know'st not what tomorrows bring:
      I wish thee well.

But thou art come, and soon or late
'Tis thine to meet the frowns of fate,
The harpy grin of envy's hate,
      And mermaid-smiles
Of worldly folly's luring bait,
      That youth beguiles.

And much I wish, whate'er may be
The lot, my child, that falls to thee,

Nature may never let thee see
      Her glass betimes,
But keep thee from my failings free—
      Nor itch at rhymes.

Lord help thee in thy coming years
If thy mad father's picture 'pears
Predominant—his feeling fears
      And jingling starts;
I'd freely now gi' vent to tears
      To ease my heart.

May thou, unknown to rhyming bother,
Be ignorant as is thy mother,
And in thy manners such another,
      Save sin's nigh guest;
And then wi' 'scaping this and t'other
      Thou mayst be blest.

Lord knows my heart, it loves thee much;
And may my feelings, aches and such,
The pains I meet in folly's clutch
      Be never thine:
Child, it's a tender string to touch,
      That sounds 'Thou'rt mine.'

Langley Bush

O Langley Bush, the shepherd's sacred shade,
    Thy hollow trunk oft gained a look from me;
Full many a journey o'er the heath I've made,
    For such-like curious things I love to see.
What truth the story of the swain allows,
    That tells of honours which thy young days knew,
Of 'Langley Court' being kept beneath thy boughs,
    I cannot tell—thus much I know is true,
That thou art reverenced: even the rude clan
    Of lawless gypsies, driven from stage to stage,
Pilfering the hedges of the husbandman,
    Spare thee, as sacred, in thy withering age.
Both swains and gypsies seem to love thy name,
    Thy spot's a favourite with the sooty crew,
And soon thou must depend on gypsy-fame,
    Thy mouldering trunk is nearly rotten through.
My last doubts murmur on the zephyr's swell,
    My last look lingers on thy boughs with pain;
To thy declining age I bid farewell,
    Like old companions, ne'er to meet again.

The Last of March
(written at Lolham Brigs)

Though o'er the darksome northern hill
    Old ambushed winter frowning flies,
And faintly drifts his threat'nings still
    In snowy sleet and blackening skies;
    Yet where the willow leaning lies
And shields beneath the budding flower,
    Where banks to break the wind arise,
'Tis sweet to sit and spend an hour.

Though floods of winter bustling fall
    Adown the arches bleak and blea,
Though snow-storms clothe the mossy wall
    And hourly whiten o'er the lea;
    Yet when from clouds the sun is free
And warms the learning bird to sing,
    'Neath sloping bank and sheltering tree
'Tis sweet to watch the creeping spring.

Though still so early, one may spy
    And track her footsteps every hour;
The daisy with its golden eye,
    And primrose bursting into flower;
    And snugly, where the thorny bower
Keeps off the nipping frost and wind,

Excluding all but sun and shower,
There children early violets find.

Here 'neath the shelving bank's retreat
   The horse-blob swells its golden ball;
Nor fear the lady-smocks to meet
   The snows that round their blossoms fall:
   Here by the arch's ancient wall
The antique eldern buds anew;
   Again the bulrush sprouting tall
The water wrinkles, rippling through.

As spring's warm herald April comes,
   As nature's sleep is nearly past,
How sweet to hear the wakening hums
   Of aught beside the winter blast!
   Of feathered minstrels first and last,
The robin's song's again begun;
   And, as skies clear when overcast,
Larks rise to hail the peeping sun.

The stirtling pewits as they pass
   Scream joyous whizzing overhead,
Right glad the fields and meadow grass
   Will quickly hide their careless shed:
   The rooks, where yonder witchens spread,
Quawk clamorous to the spring's approach;
   Here silent, from its watery bed,
To hail its coming, leaps the roach.

While stalking o'er the fields again
   In stripped defiance to the storms,
The hardy seedsman spreads the grain,
   And all his hopeful toil performs:

In flocks the timid pigeon swarms,
For scattered kernels chance may spare;
   And as the plough unbeds the worms,
The crows and magpies gather there.

Yon bullocks low their liberty,
   The young grass cropping to their fill;
And colts, from straw-yards neighing free,
   Spring's opening promise 'joy at will:
   Along the bank, beside the rill
The happy lambkins bleat and run,
   Then weary, 'neath a sheltering hill
Drop basking in the gleaming sun.

At distance from the water's edge,
   On hanging sallow's farthest stretch,
The moorhen 'gins her nest of sedge
   Safe from destroying schoolboy's reach.
   Fen-sparrows chirp and fly to fetch
The withered reed-down rustling nigh,
   And, by the sunny side the ditch,
Prepare their dwelling warm and dry.

Again a storm encroaches round,
   Thick clouds are darkening deep behind;
And through the arches hoarsely sound
   The risings of the hollow wind:
   Spring's early hopes seem half resigned
And silent for a while remain,
   Till sunbeams broken clouds can find
And brighten all to life again.

Ere yet a hailstone pattering comes,
   Or dimps the pool the rainy squall,

One hears in mighty murmuring hums
    The spirit of the tempest call:
    Here sheltering 'neath the ancient wall
I still pursue my musing dreams,
    And as the hailstones round me fall
I mark their bubbles in the streams.

Reflection here is warmed to sigh,
    Tradition gives these brigs renown,
Though heedless time long passed them by
    Nor thought them worthy noting down:
    Here in the mouth of every clown
The 'Roman road' familiar sounds;
    All else with everlasting frown
Oblivion's mantling mist surrounds.

These walls the work of Roman hands!
    How may conjecturing fancy pore,
As lonely here one calmly stands,
    On paths that age has trampled o'er.
    The builders' names are known no more;
No spot on earth their memory bears;
    And crowds, reflecting thus before,
Have since found graves as dark as theirs.

The storm has ceased—again the sun
    The ague-shivering season dries;
Short-winded March, thou'lt soon be done,
    Thy fainting tempest mildly dies.
    Soon April's flowers and dappled skies
Shall spread a couch for lovely May,
    Upon whose bosom nature lies
And smiles her joyous youth away.

To my Cottage

Thou lowly cot where first my breath I drew,
Past joys endear thee, childhood's past delight
Where each young summer's pictured on my view,
And, dearer still, the happy winter-night
When the storm pelted down with all his might
And roared and bellowed in the chimney-top
And pattered vehement 'gainst the window-light
And on the threshold fell the quick eaves-drop.
How blest I've listened on my corner stool,
Heard the storm rage, and hugged my happy spot,
While the fond parent wound her whirring spool
And spared a sigh for the poor wanderer's lot.
In thee, sweet hut, this happiness was proved,
And these endear and make thee doubly loved.

In Hilly Wood

How sweet to be thus nestling deep in boughs
Upon an ashen stoven pillowing me;
Faintly are heard the ploughmen at their ploughs,
But not an eye can find its way to see.
The sunbeams scarce molest me with a smile,
So thick the leafy armies gather round;
And where they do, the breeze blows cool the while,
Their leafy shadows dancing on the ground.
Full many a flower, too, wishing to be seen,
Perks up its head the hiding grass between—
In mid-wood silence, thus, how sweet to be,
Where all the noises that on peace intrude
Come from the chittering cricket, bird and bee,
Whose songs have charms to sweeten solitude.

To Autumn

Come, pensive autumn, with thy clouds and storms
And falling leaves and pastures lost to flowers;
A luscious charm hangs on thy faded forms,
More sweet than summer in her loveliest hours,
Who in her blooming uniform of green
Delights with samely and continued joy:
But give me, autumn, where thy hand hath been,
For there is wildness that can never cloy—
The russet hue of fields left bare, and all
The tints of leaves and blossoms ere they fall.
In thy dull days of clouds a pleasure comes,
Wild music softens in thy hollow winds,
And in thy fading woods a beauty blooms
That's more than dear to melancholy minds.

from
The Parish

[Miss Peevish Scornful]

Miss Peevish Scornful, once the village toast,
Deemed fair by some and prettyish by most,
Brought up a lady, though her father's gain
Depended still on cattle and on grain,
She followed shifting fashions and aspired
To the high notions ba·ed pride desired;
And all the profits pigs and poultry made
Were gave to Miss for dressing and parade,
To visit balls and plays, fresh hopes to chase
And try her fortune with a simpering face;
And now and then in London's crowds was shown,
To know the world and to the world be known;
All leisure hours while Miss at home sojourned
Passed in preparing till new routs returned,
Or tittle-tattling o'er her shrewd remarks
Of ladies' dresses or attentive sparks:
How Mr So-and-so at such a rout
Fixed his eyes on her all the night about,
While the good lady seated at his side
Behind her hand her blushes forced to hide
Till conscious Miss in pity she would say
'For the poor lady turned her face away!'
And young Squire Dandy, just returned from France,
How he first chose her from the rest to dance,
And at the play how such a gent resigned
His seat to her and placed himself behind;

How this squire bowed polite at her approach
And lords e'en nodded as she passed their coach.
Thus Miss in raptures would such things recall
And Pa and Ma in raptures heard it all.
But when an equal would his praise declare
And told young madam that her face was fair,
She might believe the fellow's truth the while
And just in sport might condescend to smile,
But frowned his further teasing suit to shun
And deemed it rudeness in a farmer's son.
Thus she went on, and visited and dressed,
And deemed things earnest that were spoke in jest,
And dreamed at night o'er pride's unchecked desires
Of nodding gentlemen and smiling squires.
To Gretna Green her visions often fled,
And rattling coaches lumbered in her head;
Till hopes, grown weary with too long delay,
Caught the green sickness and declined away,
And beauty, like a garment worse for wear
Fled her pale cheek and left it much too fair.
Then she gave up sick-visits, balls and plays,
Where whispers turned to anything but praise;
All were thrown by like an old-fashioned song
Where she had played show-woman much too long;
She condescended to be kind and plain,
And 'mong her equals hoped to find a swain;
Past follies now were hateful to review
And they were hated by her equals too;
Notice from equals vain she tried to court,
Or if they noticed 'twas but just in sport.
At last grown husband-mad away she ran,
Not with young Squire Dandy, but the servant man.

The Progress of Cant

Some with reform religion's shade pursue
And vote the old church wrong to join the new,
Casting away their former cold neglects,
Paying religion once a week respects,
They turn from regular old forms as bad
To pious maniacs regularly mad,
A chosen race, so their conceit would teach,
Whom cant inspired to rave and not to preach,
A set of upstarts late from darkness sprung
With this new light like mushrooms out of dung;
Though blind as owls i' the sun they lived before,
Conceit inspired and they are blind no more.
The drunken cobbler leaves his wicked life,
Hastes to save others and neglects his wife;
To mend men's souls he thinks himself designed
And leaves his shoes to the uncalled and blind;
He then like old songs runs the scriptures o'er
And makes discoveries never known before;
Makes darkest points as plain as ABC
And wonders why his hearers will not see;
Spouts facts on facts to prove that dark is light
And all are blind till he restore their sight,
And swears the old church which he cast away
As full of errors and as blind as they;
And offers prayers no doubt as prayers are cheap
For chosen shepherds to his worship's sheep;

Thinking the while, if such the will of fate,
Self might become a hopeful candidate,
And doubtless longs should reformation call
To leave his own and take his neighbour's stall.
Part urged as scripture, more as self-conceit,
To suit his ends each passage he repeats
And in as various ways each fact he weaves
As gossips' riddles upon winter eves.
Now storming threats, now pleading comforts mild,
In puling whine soft as a sucking child,
They cant and rave damnation's threats by fits
Till some old farmer loses half his wits,
Looks back on former sins, though loath to doubt,
Groans o'er a prayer and thinks himself devout.
Then learning's looked on as an idle jest,
And the old cobbler preaches far the best,
Who smooths with honeyed hopes the deep-dyed sinner
And earns reward—a lodging and a dinner.
Their former teachers as blind guides they mock,
Nor think them chosen for the crazy flock.
The crazy flock believe and are depraved,
And just in time turn idiots to be saved.

The Overseer

Art thou a man, thou tyrant o'er distress?
Doubtless thy pride would scorn to think thee less,
Then scorn a deed unworthy of that name
And live deserving of a better fame.
Hurt not the poor whom fate forbade to shine,
Whose lots were cast in meaner ways than thine,
Infringe not on the comforts they possess,
Nor bid scant hope turn hopeless in distress;
Drive not poor freedom from its niggard soil,
Its independence is their staff for toil—
Take that away which as their right they call
And thou'rt a rogue that beggars them of all.
They sink in sorrow as a race of slaves
And their last hope grows green upon their graves.
Remember, proud aspiring man of earth,
Pride's poor distinction is of mortal birth;
However high thy hated name may be,
Death in the dust shall humble pride and thee.
That hand that formed thee and lent pride its day
Took equal means to fashion humbler clay;
One power alike reigns as thy god and theirs,
Who deaf to pride gives heed to humbler prayers.
He as our father with the world began
And fashioned man in brotherhood with man;

And learn thou this, proud man, 'tis nature's creed—
Or be thou humbled if thou wilt not heed—
The kindred bond which our first father gave
Proves man thy brother still and not thy slave.

from
The Shepherd's
Calendar
(1827)

January

Dithering and keen the winter comes,
While comfort flies to close-shut rooms
And sees the snow in feathers pass
Winnowing by the window-glass,
Whilst unfelt tempests howl and beat
Above his head in chimney-seat.

Now musing o'er the changing scene,
Farmers behind the tavern-screen
Collect—with elbow idly pressed
On hob reclines the corner's guest,
Reading the news, to mark again
The bankrupt lists or price of grain,
Or old Moore's annual prophecies
Of flooded fields and clouded skies,
Whose Almanac's thumbed pages swarm
With frost and snow and many a storm,
And wisdom gossiped from the stars,
Of politics and bloody wars.
He shakes his head and still proceeds,
Nor doubts the truth of what he reads:
All wonders are with faith supplied—
Bible at once and weather-guide.
Puffing the while his red-tipped pipe,

He dreams o'er troubles nearly ripe;
Yet not quite lost in profit's way
He'll turn to next year's harvest-day,
And, winter's leisure to regale,
Hope better times and—sip his ale.

The schoolboy still with dithering joys
In pastime leisure hours employs,
And, be the weather as it may,
Is never at a loss for play:
Making rude forms of various names,
Snowmen or aught his fancy frames,
Till numbed and shivering he resorts
To brisker games and warmer sports—
Kicking with many a flying bound
The football o'er the frozen ground,
Or seeking bright glib ice to play
And slide the wintry hours away,
As quick and smooth as shadows run
When clouds in autumn pass the sun.
Some, hurrying rambles eager take
To skate upon the meadow lake,
Scaring the snipe from her retreat,
From shelving bank's unfrozen seat
Or running brook where icy spars
Which the pale sunlight specks with stars
Shoot crizzling o'er the restless tide,
To many a likeness petrified;
The moorhen, too, with fear oppressed
Starts from her reedy sheltered rest,
As skating by with curving springs
And arms outspread like heron's wings,

They race away for pleasure's sake
With hunter's speed along the lake.

Blackening through the evening sky,
In clouds the starlings daily fly
To Whittlesea's reed-wooded mere
And osier holts by rivers near,
Whilst many a mingled swarthy crowd—
Rook, crow and jackdaw—noising loud,
Fly to and fro to dreary fen,
Dull winter's weary flight again;
They flop on heavy wings away
As soon as morning wakens grey
And when the sun sets round and red
Return to naked woods to bed.

The sun is creeping out of sight
Behind the woods—whilst running night
Hastens to shut the day's dull eye
And grizzle o'er the chilly sky.
Now maidens fresh as summer roses,
Journeying from the distant closes,
Haste home with yokes and swinging pail;
The thresher, too, sets by his flail
And leaves the mice at peace again
To fill their holes with stolen grain,
Whilst owlets, glad his toils are o'er,
Swoop by him as he shuts the door.

Bearing his hook beneath his arm,
The shepherd seeks the cottage warm;
And, weary in the cold to roam,

Scenting the track that leads him home,
His dog with swifter pace proceeds
And barks to urge his master's speed,
Then turns and looks him in the face
And trots before with mending pace
Till, out of whistle from the swain,
He sits him down and barks again,
Anxious to greet the opened door
And meet the cottage-fire once more.

The shutter closed, the lamp alight,
The faggot chopped and blazing bright—
The shepherd now from labour free
Dances his children on his knee,
While underneath his master's seat
The tired dog lies in slumbers sweet,
Starting and whimpering in his sleep,
Chasing still the straying sheep.
The cat's rolled round in vacant chair
Or leaping children's knees to lair—
Or purring on the warmer hearth,
Sweet chorus to the cricket's mirth.

The redcap hanging overhead
In cage of wire is perched a-bed,
Slumbering in his painted feathers,
Unconscious of the out-door weathers:
Ev'n things without the cottage walls
Meet comfort as the evening falls—
As happy in the winter's dearth
As those around the blazing hearth—
The ass (frost-driven from the moor

Where storms through naked bushes roar
And not a leaf or sprig of green
On ground or quaking bush is seen,
Save grey-veined ivy's hardy pride
Round old trees by the common side)
Littered with straw, now dozes warm,
Beneath his shed, from snow and storm;
The swine are fed and in the sty
And fowls snug perched in hovel nigh
With head in feathers safe asleep,
Where fox find ne'er a hole to creep;
And geese are gabbling in their dreams
Of littered corn and thawing streams.
The sparrow too, a daily guest,
Is in the cottage eaves at rest;
And robin small and smaller wren
Are in their warm holes safe again
From falling snows that winnow by
The hovels where they nightly lie,
And ague winds that shake the tree
Where other birds are forced to be.

The housewife, busy night and day,
Clears the supper-things away;
The jumping cat starts from her seat;
And stretching up on weary feet
The dog wakes at the welcome tones
That call him up to pick the bones.

On corner walls, a glittering row,
Hang fire-irons—less for use than show,
With horse-shoe brightened, as a spell,

Witchcraft's evil powers to quell;
And warming-pan, reflecting bright
The crackling blaze's flickering light,
That hangs the corner wall to grace,
Nor oft is taken from its place—
Yet still 'tis bright as gold can be,
And children often peep to see
Their laughing faces as they pass
Gleam on the lid as plain as glass.

Supper removed, the mother sits
And tells her tales by starts and fits.
Not willing to lose time or toil,
She knits or sews and talks the while
Something that may be warnings found
To the young listeners gaping round—
Of boys who in her early day
Strolled to the meadow-lake to play,
Where willows o'er the bank inclined
Sheltered the water from the wind
And left it scarcely crizzled o'er—
When one plopped in, to rise no more!
And how, upon a market-night,
When not a star bestowed its light,
A farmer's shepherd, o'er his glass,
Forgot that he had woods to pass:
And having sold his master's sheep,
Was overta'en by darkness deep.
How, coming with his startled horse,
To where two roads a hollow cross,
Where, lone guide when a stranger strays,
A white post points four different ways,

Beside the wood-ride's lonely gate
A murdering robber lay in wait.
The frightened horse with broken rein
Stood at the stable-door again,
But none came home to fill his rack
Or take the saddle from his back:
The saddle it was all he bore—
The man was seen alive no more!
In her young days, beside the wood
The gibbet in its terror stood:
Though now all gone, 'tis not forgot,
But dreaded as a haunted spot.

She from her memory oft repeats
Witches' dread powers and fairy feats:
How one has oft been known to prance
In cow-cribs like a coach to France
And ride on sheep-trays from the fold,
At racehorse speed to Burton-hold,
To join the midnight mystery's rout
Where witches meet the yews about;
And how, when met with unawares,
They turn at once to cats or hares
And race along with hellish flight,
Now here, now there, now out of sight!
And how the other tiny things
Will leave their moonlight meadow-rings
And unperceived through key-holes creep,
When all around have sunk to sleep,
To feast on what the cotter leaves—
Mice are not reckoned greater thieves.
They take away as well as eat

And still the housewife's eye they cheat
In spite of all the folks that swarm
In cottage small and larger farm—
They through each key-hole pop and pop
Like wasps into a grocer's shop,
With all the things that they can win
From chance to put their plunder in,
As shells of walnuts, split in two
By crows who with the kernels flew,
Or acorn-cups by stock doves plucked,
Or eggshells by a cuckoo sucked.
With broad leaves of the sycamore
They clothe their stolen dainties o'er:
And when in cellar they regale,
Bring hazel-nuts to hold their ale,
With bung-holes bored by squirrels well
To get the kernel from the shell,
Or maggots a way out to win,
When all is gone that grew within.
And be the key-holes e'er so high,
Rush poles a ladder's help supply,
Where soft the climbers fearless tread
On spindles made of spiders' thread.
And foul or fair or dark the night,
Their wild-fire lamps are burning bright:
For which full many a daring crime
Is acted in the summer-time—
When glow-worm found in lanes remote
Is murdered for its shining coat
And put in flowers that nature weaves
With hollow shapes and silken leaves,
Such as the Canterbury bell,
Serving for lamp or lantern well;

Or, following with unwearied watch
The flight of one they cannot match,
As silence sliveth upon sleep
Or thieves by dozing watch-dogs creep,
They steal from Jack-a-Lantern's tails
A light whose guidance never fails
To aid them in the darkest night
And guide their plundering steps aright.
Rattling away in printless tracks,
Some horsed on beetles' glossy backs
Go whisking on—and others hie
As fast as loaded moths can fly:
Some urge, the morning cock to shun,
The hardest gallop mice can run,
In chariots, lolling at their ease,
Made of whate'er their fancies please
Things that in childhood's memory dwell—
Scooped crow-pot-stone or cockle-shell,
With wheels at hand of mallow seeds,
Where childish sport was stringing beads;
And thus equipped they softly pass
Like shadows on the summer grass
And glide away in troops together,
Just as the spring-wind drives a feather.
As light as happy dreams they creep,
Nor break the feeblest link of sleep:
A midgeon, in their road a-bed,
Feels not the wheels run o'er his head,
But sleeps till sunrise calls him up,
Unconscious of the passing troop.

　　Thus dame the winter-night regales
With wonder's never-ceasing tales;

While in a corner, ill at ease,
Or crushing 'tween their father's knees,
The children—silent all the while,
And e'en repressed the laugh or smile—
Quake with the ague chills of fear
And tremble though they love to hear,
Starting while they the tales recall
At their own shadows on the wall,
Till the old clock, that strikes unseen
Behind the picture-pasted screen
Where Eve and Adam still agree
To rob Life's fatal apple-tree,
Counts over bedtime's hour of rest
And bids each be sleep's fearful guest.
She then her half-told tales will leave
To finish on tomorrow's eve.
The children steal away to bed
And up the ladder softly tread,
Scarce daring—from their fearful joys—
To look behind or make a noise,
Nor speak a word. But still as sleep
They secret to their pillows creep
And whisper o'er in terror's way
The prayers they dare no louder say,
Then hide their heads beneath the clothes
And try in vain to seek repose,
While yet, to fancy's sleepless eye,
Witches on sheep-trays gallop by
And fairies like to rising sparks,
Swarm twittering round them in the dark,
Till sleep creeps nigh to ease their cares
And drops upon them unawares.

O spirit of the days gone by—
Sweet childhood's fearful ecstasy!
The witching spells of winter nights,
Where are they fled with their delights,
When list'ning on the corner seat,
The winter evening's length to cheat,
I heard my mother's memory tell
Tales superstition loves so well,
Things said or sung a thousand times,
In simple prose or simpler rhymes?
Ah, where is page of poesy
So sweet as theirs was wont to be?
The magic wonders that deceived
When fictions were as truths believed,
The fairy feats that once prevailed
Told to delight and never failed:
Where are they now, their fears and sighs,
And tears from founts of happy eyes?
I read in books but find them not,
For poesy hath its youth forgot;
I hear them told to children still,
But fear numbs not my spirits chill;
I still see faces pale with dread
While mine could laugh at what is said,
See tears imagined woes supply
While mine with real cares are dry.
Where are they gone, the joys and fears,
The links, the life of other years?
I thought they twined around my heart
So close that we could never part,
But reason like a winter's day
Nipped childhood's visions all away,

Nor left behind one withering flower
To cherish in a lonely hour.
Memory may yet the themes repeat,
But childhood's heart hath ceased to beat
At tales which reason's sterner lore
Turns like weak gossips from her door:
The Magic Fountain, where the head
Rose up just as the startled maid
Was stooping from the weedy brink
To dip her pitcher in to drink,
That did its half-hid mystery tell
To smooth its hair and use it well,
Which, doing as it bade her do,
Turned to a king and lover too.
The tale of Cinderella told
The winter through and never old:
The pumpkin that at her approach
Was turned into a golden coach;
The rats that fairies' magic knew
And instantly to horses grew;
The coachmen ready at her call
To drive her to the Prince's ball,
With fur-changed jackets silver-lined
And tails hung 'neath their hats behind;
The golden glove with fingers small
She lost while dancing in the hall,
That was on every finger tried
And fitted hers and none beside,
When Cinderella, soon as seen,
Was wooed and won, and made a queen.
The boy that did the giant slay
And gave his mother's cows away

For magic mask that day or night
When on would keep him out of sight.
The running beans—not such as weaves
Round poles the height of cottage eaves,
But magic ones that travelled high
Some steeple's journey up the sky
And reached a giant's dwelling there,
A cloud-built castle in the air,
Where, venturing up the fearful height,
That served him climbing half the night,
He searched the giant's coffers o'er
And never wanted riches more,
While, like a lion scenting food,
The giant roared in hungry mood
A storm of threats that might suffice
To freeze the hottest blood to ice.

　　I hear it now, nor dream of harm;
The storm is settled to a calm.
Those fears are dead—what will not die
In fading life's mortality?
Those truths have fled and left behind
A real world and doubting mind.

from March

March, month of 'many weathers', wildly comes
In hail and snow and rain and threatening hums
And floods—while often at his cottage-door
The shepherd stands to hear the distant roar
Loosed from the rushing mills and river-locks
With thundering sound and overpowering shocks.
From bank to bank along the meadow lea
The river spreads and shines a little sea,
While in the pale sunlight a watery brood
Of swopping white birds flock about the flood.
. . . .

    The shepherd-boy, that hastens now and then
From hail and snow beneath his sheltering den
Of flags or file-leaved sedges tied in sheaves
Or stubble shocks, oft as his eye perceives
Sun-threads shrink out in momentary smiles,
With fancy thoughts his loneliness beguiles,
Thinking the struggling winter hourly by,
As down the edges of the distant sky
The hailstorm sweeps—and while he stops to strip
The stooping hedge-briar of its lingering hip,
He hears the wild geese gabble o'er his head,
Then, pleased with fancies in his musings bred,
He marks the figured forms in which they fly
And pausing, follows with a wondering eye,

Likening their curious march in curves or rows
To every letter which his memory knows,
While, far above, the solitary crane
Swings lonely to unfrozen dykes again,
Cranking a jarring melancholy cry
Through the wild journey of the cheerless sky.

from May

The driving boy beside his team
Of May-month beauty now will dream
And cock his hat and turn his eye
On flower and tree and deepening sky,
And oft burst loud in fits of song
And whistle as he reels along,
Cracking his whip in starts of joy—
A happy, dirty, driving boy.
The youth who leaves his corner stool
Betimes for neighbouring village-school,
Where as a mark to guide him right
The church spire's all the way in sight,
With cheerings from his parents given,
Starts 'neath the joyous smiles of heaven
And sawns with many an idle stand,
With book-bag swinging in his hand,
And gazes as he passes by
On every thing that meets his eye.
Young lambs seem tempting him to play,
Dancing and bleating in his way—
With trembling tails and pointed ears
They follow him and lose their fears;
He smiles upon their sunny faces
And fain would join their happy races.

The birds that sing on bush and tree
Seem chirping for his company;
And all—in fancy's idle whim—
Seem keeping holiday, but him.
He lolls upon each resting stile
To see the fields so sweetly smile,
To see the wheat grow green and long,
And lists the weeder's toiling song
Or short note of the changing thrush
Above him in the whitethorn bush
That o'er the leaning stile bends low
Loaded with mockery of snow.

from June

The mowing gangs bend o'er the beaded grass,
Where oft the gypsy's hungry journeying ass
Will turn its wishes from the meadow paths,
List'ning the rustle of the falling swaths.
The ploughman sweats along the fallow vales
And down the sun-cracked furrow slowly trails,
Oft seeking when athirst the brook's supply
Where, brushing eager the brink's bushes by
For coolest water, he disturbs the rest
Of ring-dove brooding o'er its idle nest.
The shepherd's leisure hours are over now;
No more he loiters 'neath the hedge-row bough
On shadow-pillowed banks and lolling stile;
The wilds must lose their summer friend awhile.
With whistle, barking dogs and chiding scold,
He drives the bleating sheep from fallow fold
To wash-pools where the willow shadows lean,
Dashing them in, their fold-stained coats to clean;
Then on the sunny sward when dry again,
He brings them homeward to the clipping pen,
Of hurdles formed, where elm or sycamore
Shut out the sun—or to some threshing-floor.
There with the scraps of songs and laugh and tale,
They lighten annual toil while merry ale

Goes round and glads some old man's heart to praise
The threadbare customs of the bygone days:
How the huge bowl was in the middle set
At breakfast time, when clippers yearly met,
Filled full of furmety, where dainty swum
The streaking sugar and the spotting plum,
Which maids could never to the table bring
Without one rising from the merry ring
To lend a hand, who, if 'twas ta'en amiss,
Would sell his kindness for a stolen kiss.
The large stone pitcher in its homely trim
And clouded pint-horn with its copper rim
Were there, from which were drunk with spirits high
Healths of the best the cellar could supply,
While sung the ancient swains in uncouth rhymes
Songs that were pictures of the good old times.
Thus will the old man ancient ways bewail,
Till toiling shears gain ground upon the tale
And break it off—for now the timid sheep,
His fleece shorn off, starts with a fearful leap,
Shaking his naked skin with wond'ring joys,
While others are brought in by sturdy boys.

from July
[*manuscript version*]

Daughter of pastoral smells & sights
& sultry days & dewy nights
July resumes her yearly place
Wi her milking maiden face
Ruddy & tannd yet sweet to view
When everyweres a veil of dew
& raps it round her looks that smiles
a lovly rest to daily toils
wi last months closing scenes & dins
her sultry beaming birth begins
Hay makers still in grounds appear
& some are thinning nearly clear
Save oddling lingering shocks about
Which the tithman counteth out
Sticking their green boughs were they go
The parsons yearly claims to know
Which farmers view wi grudging eye
& grumbling drive their waggons bye
In hedge bound close & meadow plains
Stript groups of busy bustling swains
From all her haunts wi noises rude
Drives to the wood lands solitude
That seeks a spot unmarkd wi paths
Far from the close & meadow swaths

Wi smutty song & story gay
They cart the withered smelling hay
Boys loading on the waggon stand
& men below wi sturdy hand
Heave up the shocks on lathy prong
While horse boys lead the team along
& maidens drag the rake behind
Wi light dress shaping to the wind
& trembling locks of curly hair
& snow white bosoms nearly bare
That charms ones sight amid the hay
Like lingering blossoms of the may.
From clowns rude jokes the[y] often turn
& oft their cheeks wi blushes burn
From talk which to escape a sneer
They oft affect as not to hear

from September

    Anon the fields are nearly clear
And glad sounds hum in labour's ear,
When children halloo 'Here they come!'
And run to meet the Harvest Home,
Stuck thick with boughs and thronged with boys,
Who mingle loud a merry noise,
And when they meet the stack-thronged yard
Cross-buns and pence their shouts reward.
Then comes the harvest-supper night,
Which rustics welcome with delight,
When merry game and tiresome tale
And songs increasing with the ale
Their mingled uproar interpose
To crown the harvest's happy close,
While rural mirth that there abides
Laughs till she almost cracks her sides.

from October
[*manuscript draft*]

The flying cloud the gusts of sudden wind
Which prophecy encroaching storms behind
                                        lea
Fluttering the sear leaves oer the bleaching grass
That litters under every fading tree
& pausing oft as falls the patting rain
Then gathering strength & twirling them again
                                        hurried
The startld stockdove hurriying wizzing bye
                                        the sky
As the still hawk hangs oer him in dusk
                                        as they
Crows from the oaks trees qawking flusk spring
Dashing the acorns down wi beating wing
Waking the woodlands sleep in noises low
Wafting the stillness of the woods
Patting the crimpt brakes withering brown below
                        jackdaws
The crows and daws flapping home at night
                        in
& puddock circling round its lazy flight
Round the wild sweeing wood in motion slow
Before it perches on the oaks below

& hugh black beetles revelling alone
                        their
In the dull evening wi its heavy drone
Buzzing from barn door dung & hovel sides
Were fodderd cattel from the night abides
. . . .

Autum
Spring once met plains that stretchd them far away
In uncheckt shadows of green brown & grey
Unbounded freedom ruld the wandering scene
No fence of ownership crept in between
To hide the prospect from the gazing eye
Its only bondage was the circling sky
A mighty flat undwarfd by bush & tree
Spread its feint shadow of imensity
& lost itself which seemd to eke its bounds
In the blue mist the orisons edge surrounds
Now this sweet visions of my boyish hours
Free as spring clouds & wild as forest flowers
                        hope
Is faded all a thought that blossomd free
& hath been once all it no more shall be
Inclosure came & trampld on the grave
Of labours rights & left the poor a slave
& memorys pride ere want to wealth did bow
Is both the shadow & the substance now
The sheep & cows were free to range as then
Were change might prompt nor felt the bonds of men
Cows went & came wi every morn & night
To the wild pasture as their common right
                                rising
& sheep unfolded wi the morning sun

Heard the swains shout & felt their freedom won
Trackd the red fallow field & heath & plain
Or sought the brook to drink & roamd again
While the glad shepherd tracd their tracks along
Free as the lark & happy as her song
But now alls fled & flats of many a dye
That seemd to lengthen wi the following eye
Mores loosing from the sight far smooth & blea
Were swopt the plover in its pleasure free
Are vanished now with heaths once wild & gay
As poets visions of lifes early day
Like mighty jiants of their limbs bereft
The sky bound wastes in mangld garbs are left
Fence meeting fence in owners little bounds
Of field & meadow large as garden grounds
In little parcels little minds to please
Leave men & flocks imprisond ill at ease
For with the poor stern freedom bade farwell
& fortune hunters totter were they fell
                    riches
They dreamd of weath in the rebel scheme
& find too truly that they did but dream

from December

Glad Christmas comes and every hearth
    Makes room to give him welcome now,
E'en want will dry its tears in mirth
    And crown him with a holly bough;
Though tramping 'neath a winter sky
    O'er snowy paths and rimy stiles,
The housewife sets her spinning by
    To bid him welcome with her smiles.

Each house is swept the day before,
    And windows stuck with evergreens,
The snow is besomed from the door
    And comfort crowns the cottage scenes.
Gilt holly with its thorny pricks
    And yew and box with berries small,
These deck the unused candlesticks
    And pictures hanging by the wall.

Neighbours resume their annual cheer,
    Wishing, with smiles and spirits high,
Glad Christmas and a happy year,
    To every morning passer-by;
Milkmaids their Christmas journeys go,
    Accompanied with favoured swain;

And children pace the crumping snow
    To taste their granny's cake again.

The shepherd, now no more afraid,
    Since custom doth the chance bestow,
Starts up to kiss the giggling maid
    Beneath the branch of mistletoe
That 'neath each cottage beam is seen
    With pearl-like berries shining gay,
The shadow still of what hath been,
    Which fashion yearly fades away.

And singers too, a merry throng,
    At early morn with simple skill
Yet imitate the angels' song
    And chant their Christmas ditty still;
And—'mid the storm that dies and swells
    By fits—in hummings softly steals
The music of the village bells,
    Ringing round their merry peals.

When this is past, a merry crew
    Bedecked in masks and ribbons gay,
The 'Morris-dance,' their sports renew
    And act their winter evening play.
The clown turned king for penny-praise
    Storms with the actor's strut and swell,
And Harlequin a laugh to raise
    Wears his hunch-back and tinkling bell.

And oft for pence and spicy ale,
    With winter nosegays pinned before,

The wassail-singer tells her tale
    And drawls her Christmas carols o'er,
While 'prentice boy with ruddy face
    And rime-bepowdered dancing locks
From door to door with happy pace
    Runs round to claim his 'Christmas box.'
. . . .

Old customs! O I love the sound,
    However simple they may be—
Whate'er with time hath sanction found
    Is welcome and is dear to me—
Pride grows above simplicity
    And spurns them from her haughty mind,
And soon the poet's song will be
    The only refuge they can find.

The Moors

Far spread the moory ground, a level scene
Bespread with rush and one eternal green
That never felt the rage of blundering plough
Though centuries wreathed spring's blossoms on its brow,
Still meeting plains that stretched them far away
In unchecked shadows of green, brown and grey.
Unbounded freedom ruled the wandering scene
Nor fence of ownership crept in between
To hide the prospect of the following eye—
Its only bondage was the circling sky.
One mighty flat undwarfed by bush and tree
Spread its faint shadow of immensity
And lost itself, which seemed to eke its bounds,
In the blue mist the horizon's edge surrounds.
Now this sweet vision of my boyish hours,
Free as spring clouds and wild as summer flowers,
Is faded all—a hope that blossomed free,
And hath been once, no more shall ever be.
Enclosure came and trampled on the grave
Of labour's rights and left the poor a slave,
And memory's pride, ere want to wealth did bow,
Is both the shadow and the substance now.
The sheep and cows were free to range as then
Where change might prompt, nor felt the bonds of men:

Cows went and came with evening, morn and night
To the wild pasture as their common right,
And sheep unfolded with the rising sun
Heard the swains shout and felt their freedom won,
Tracked the red fallow field and heath and plain,
Then met the brook and drank and roamed again—
The brook that dribbled on as clear as glass
Beneath the roots they hid among the grass—
While the glad shepherd traced their tracks along,
Free as the lark and happy as her song.
But now all's fled and flats of many a dye
That seemed to lengthen with the following eye,
Moors losing from the sight, far, smooth and blea,
Where swopt the plover in its pleasure free,
Are vanished now with commons wild and gay
As poets' visions of life's early day.
Mulberry bushes where the boy would run
To fill his hands with fruit are grubbed and done,
And hedgerow briars—flower-lovers overjoyed
Came and got flower pots—these are all destroyed,
And sky-bound moors in mangled garbs are left
Like mighty giants of their limbs bereft.
Fence now meets fence in owners' little bounds
Of field and meadow, large as garden grounds,
In little parcels little minds to please
With men and flocks imprisoned, ill at ease.
Each little path that led its pleasant way
As sweet as morning leading night astray,
Where little flowers bloomed round, a varied host,
That Travel felt delighted to be lost
Nor grudged the steps that he had ta'en as vain
When right roads traced his journey's end again;

Nay on a broken tree he'd sit awhile
To see the moors and fields and meadows smile,
Sometimes with cowslips smothered—then all white
With daisies—then the summer's splendid sight
Of corn fields crimson o'er, the 'headache' bloomed
Like splendid armies for the battle plumed;
He gazed upon them with wild fancy's eye
As fallen landscapes from an evening sky.
These paths are stopped—the rude philistine's thrall
Is laid upon them and destroyed them all.
Each little tyrant with his little sign
Shows where man claims, earth glows no more divine.
On paths to freedom and to childhood dear
A board sticks up to notice 'no road here'
And on the tree with ivy overhung
The hated sign by vulgar taste is hung
As though the very birds should learn to know
When they go there they must no further go.
Thus, with the poor, scared freedom bade good-bye
And much they feel it in the smothered sigh,
And birds and trees and flowers without a name
All sighed when lawless law's enclosure came,
And dreams of plunder in such rebel schemes
Have found too truly that they were but dreams.

from
The Midsummer Cushion

Shadows of Taste

Taste with as many hues doth hearts engage
As leaves and flowers do upon nature's page;
Not mind alone the instinctive mood declares,
But birds and flowers and insects are its heirs—
Taste is their joyous heritage and they
All choose for joy in a peculiar way.
Birds own it in the various spots they choose:
Some live content in low grass gemmed with dews;
The yellowhammer like a tasteful guest
'Neath picturesque green molehills makes a nest,
Where oft the shepherd with unlearned ken
Finds strange eggs scribbled as with ink and pen—
He looks with wonder on the learned marks
And calls them in his memory writing larks;
Birds bolder-winged on bushes love to be,
While some choose cradles on the highest tree—
There rocked by winds they feel no moods of fear
But joy, their birthright, lives for ever near;
And the bold eagle, which man's fear enshrouds,
Would, could he lodge it, house upon the clouds;
While little wrens, mistrusting none that come,
In each low hovel meet a sheltered home.
Flowers in the wisdom of creative choice
Seem blest with feeling and a silent voice:

Some on the barren roads delight to bloom
And others haunt the melancholy tomb
Where death, the blight of all, finds summer's hours
Too kind to miss him with her host of flowers;
Some flourish in the sun and some the shade;
Who almost in his morning smiles would fade,
These in leaf-darkened woods right timid stray
And in its green night smile their lives away;
Others in water live and scarcely seem
To peep their little flowers above the stream,
While water lilies in their glories come
And spread green isles of beauty round their home.
All share the summer's glory and its good,
And taste of joy in each peculiar mood.
Insects of varied taste in rapture share
The heyday luxuries which she comes to heir;
In wild disorder various routs they run
In water, earth, still shade and busy sun;
And in the crowd of green earth's busy claims
They e'en grow nameless mid so many names.
And man, that noble insect, restless man
Whose thoughts scale heaven in its mighty span,
Pours forth his living soul in many a shade
And taste runs riot in her every grade.
While the low herd, mere savages subdued,
With nought of feeling or of taste imbued
Pass over sweetest scenes a careless eye
As blank as midnight in its deepest dye;
From these, and different far in rich degrees,
Minds spring as various as the leaves of trees
To follow taste and all her sweets explore
And Edens make where deserts spread before.

In poesy's spells some all their raptures find
And revel in the melodies of mind;
There nature o'er the soul her beauty flings
In all the sweets and essences of things—
A face of beauty in a city crowd
Met, passed, and vanished like a summer cloud,
In poesy's vision more refined and fair
Taste reads o'erjoyed and greets her image there.
Dashes of sunshine and a page of may
Live there a whole life long one summer's day;
A blossom in its witchery of bloom
There gathered dwells in beauty and perfume;
The singing bird, the brook that laughs along,
There ceaseless sing and never thirsts for song.
A pleasing image to its page conferred
In living character and breathing word
Becomes a landscape heard and felt and seen,
Sunshine and shade one harmonising green
Where meads and brooks and forests basking lie,
Lasting as truth and the eternal sky.
Thus truth to nature, as the true sublime,
Stands a Mount Atlas overpeering time.
    Styles may with fashions vary—tawdry, chaste,
Have had their votaries which each fancied taste:
From Donne's old homely gold whose broken feet
Jostles the reader's patience from its seat
To Pope's smooth rhymes that regularly play
In music's stated periods all the way
That starts and closes, starts again and chimes
Its tuning gamut true as minster chimes.
From these old fashions stranger metres flow,
Half prose, half verse, that stagger as they go;

One line starts smooth and then for room perplexed
Elbows along and knocks against the next
And half its neighbour—where a pause marks time,
There the clause ends—what follows is for rhyme.
Yet truth to nature will in all remain
As grass in winter glorifies the plain,
And over fashion's foils rise proud and high
As light's bright fountain in a cloudy sky.
    The man of science in discovery's moods
Roams o'er the furze-clad heath, leaf-buried woods,
And by the simple brook in rapture finds
Treasures that wake the laugh of vulgar hinds
Who see no further in his dark employs
Than village childern seeking after toys—
Their clownish hearts and ever heedless eyes
Find nought in nature they as wealth can prize,
With them self-interest and the thoughts of gain
Are nature's beauties: all beside are vain.
But he, the man of science and of taste,
Sees wealth far richer in the worthless waste
Where bits of lichen and a sprig of moss
Will all the raptures of his mind engross
And bright-winged insects on the flowers of May
Shine pearls too wealthy to be cast away—
His joys run riot mid each juicy blade
Of grass where insects revel in the shade.
And minds of different moods will oft condemn
His taste as cruel—such the deeds to them,
While he unconscious gibbets butterflies
And strangles beetles all to make us wise.
Taste's rainbow visions own unnumbered hues
And every shade its sense of taste pursues.

The heedless mind may laugh, the clown may stare,
They own no soul to look for pleasure there;
Their grosser feelings in a coarser dress
Mock at the wisdom which they can't possess.
     Some in recordless rapture love to breathe
Nature's wild Eden, wood and field and heath;
In common blades of grass his thoughts will raise
A world of beauty to admire and praise
Until his heart o'erflows with swarms of thought
To that great being who raised life from nought;
The common weed adds graces to his mind
And gleams in beauty few beside may find—
Associations sweet each object breeds
And fine ideas upon fancy feeds;
He loves not flowers because they shed perfumes
Or butterflies alone for painted plumes
Or birds for singing, although sweet it be,
But he doth love the wild and meadow lea—
There hath the flower its dwelling place and there
The butterfly goes dancing through the air;
He loves each desolate neglected spot
That seems in labour's hurry left forgot,
The warped and punished trunk of stunted oak
Freed from its bonds but by the thunder-stroke,
As cramped by straggling ribs of ivy sere—
There the glad bird makes home for half the year.
But take these several beings from their homes,
Each beauteous thing a withered thought becomes,
Association fades and like a dream
They are but shadows of the things they seem;
Torn from their homes and happiness they stand
The poor dull captives of a foreign land.

Some spruce and delicate ideas feed:
With them disorder is an ugly weed
And wood and heath a wilderness of thorns
Which gardener's shears nor fashions nor adorns;
No spots give pleasure so forlorn and bare
But gravel walks would work rich wonders there—
With such, wild nature's beauties run to waste
And art's strong impulse mars the truth of taste.
Such are the various moods that taste displays,
Surrounding wisdom in concentring rays
Where threads of light from one bright focus run
As day's proud halo circles round the sun.

Childhood

The past it is a magic word
Too beautiful to last,
It looks back like a lovely face—
Who can forget the past?
There's music in its childhood
That's known in every tongue,
Like the music of the wildwood
All chorus to the song.

The happy dream, the joyous play,
The life without a sigh,
The beauty thoughts can ne'er portray,
In those four letters lie;
The painter's beauty-breathing arts,
The poet's speaking pens,
Can ne'er call back a thousand part
Of what that word contains.

And fancy at its sweetest hour
What e'er may come to pass
Shall find that magic thrill no more—
Time broke it like his glass.
The sweetest joy, the fairest face,
The treasure most preferred,

Have left the honours of their place
Locked in that silent word.

When we look back on what we were
And feel what we are now,
A fading leaf is not so drear
Upon a broken bough,
A winter seat without a fire,
A cold world without friends
Doth not such chilly glooms impart
As that one word portends.

Like withered wreaths in banquet halls
When all the rout is past,
Like sunshine that on ruins falls
Our pleasures are at last;
The joy is fled, the love is cold,
And beauty's splendour too;
Our first believings all are old
And faith itself untrue.

When beauty met love's budding spring
In artless witcheries,
It were not then an earthly thing
But an angel in disguise;
Where are they now of youth's esteems?
All shadows past away,
Flowers blooming but in summer dreams
And thoughts of yesterday.

Our childhood soon a trifle gets
Yet like a broken toy
Grown out of date it recollects
Our memories into joy;

The simple catalogue of things
That reason would despise
Starts in the heart a thousand springs
Of half-forgotten joys.

When we review that place of prime
That childhood's joys endow,
That seemed more green in winter time
Than summer grass does now,
Where oft the task of skill was put
For other boys to match,
To run along the churchyard wall
Or balls to cuck and catch.

How oft we clomb the porch to cut
Our names upon the leads,
Though fame nor anything akin
Was never in our heads,
Where hands and feet were rudely drawn
And names we could not spell,
And thought no artist in the world
Could ever do as well.

We twirled our tops that spun so well
They scarce could tumble down,
And thought they twirled as well again
When riddled on the crown;
And bee-spell marbles bound to win
As by a potent charm
Was often wetted in the mouth
To show the dotted swarm.

We pelted at the weathercock
And he who pelted o'er

Was reckoned as a mighty man
And even something more;
We leapt across 'cat gallows sticks'
And mighty proud was he
Who overshot the famous nicks
That reached above his knee.

And then each other's tasks we did
And great ambition grew;
We ran so swift, so strong we leaped,
We almost thought we flew;
We ran across the broken brig
Whose wooden rail was lost
And loud the victor's feat was hailed
Who dared the danger most.

And hopscotch too, a spur to joy,
We thought the task divine
To hop and kick the stone right out
And never touch a line;
And then we walked on mighty stilts
Scarce seven inches high,
Yet on we stalked and thought ourselves
Already at the sky.

Our pride to reason would not shrink
In these exalted hours,
A giant's was a pigmy link
To statures such as ours;
We even fancied we could fly
And fancy then was true,
So with the clouds upon the sky
In dreams at night we flew.

We shot our arrows from our bows
Like any archers proud
And thought when lost they went so high
To lodge upon a cloud;
And these seemed feats that none before
Ourselves could e'er attain
And Wellington with all his feats
Felt never half so vain.

And oft we urged the barking dog,
For mischief was our glee,
To chase the cat up weed-green walls
And mossy apple tree;
When her tail stood like a bottle-brush
With fear—we laughed again;
Like tyrants we could purchase mirth
And ne'er allow for pain.

And then our play pots sought and won
For uses and for show
That Wedgwood's self with all his skill
Might guess in vain to know;
And palaces of stone and stick
In which we could not creep,
Which Nash himself ne'er made so quick
And never half so cheap.

Our fancies made us great and rich,
No bounds our wealth could fix,
A stool drawn round the room was soon
A splendid coach and six;
The magic of our minds was great
And even pebbles they

Soon as we chose to call them gold
Grew guineas in our play.

And carriages of oyster shells,
Though filled with nought but stones,
Grew instant ministers of state
While clay kings filled their thrones;
Like Cinderella's fairy queen
Joy would our wants bewitch:
If wealth was sought, the dust and stones
Turned wealth and made us rich.

The mallow seed became a cheese,
The henbanes loaves of bread,
A burdock leaf our table cloth
On a table stone was spread;
The bindweed flower that climbs the hedge
Made us a drinking glass,
And there we spread our merry feast
Upon the summer grass.

A henbane root could scarcely grow,
A mallow shake its seeds,
The insects that might feed thereon
Found famine in the weeds,
But like the pomp of princely taste
That humbler life annoys
We thought not of our neighbours' wants
While we were wasting joys.

We often tried to force the snail
To leave his harvest horn
By singing that the beggar-man
Was coming for his corn;

We thought we forced the ladycow
To tell the time of day:
'Twas one o'clock and two o'clock
And then she flew away.

We bawled to beetles as they ran
That their childern were all gone,
Their houses down and door key hid
Beneath the golden stone;
They seemed to haste as fast again
While we shouted as they past
With mirth half-mad to think our tale
Had urged their speed so fast.

The stonecrop that on ruins comes
And hangs like golden balls,
How oft to reach its shining blooms
We scaled the mossy walls.
And weeds—we gathered weeds as well
Of all that bore a flower
And tied our little posies up
Beneath the eldern bower.

Right eagerly our eyes would stoop
For makeshift stones for taws,
And bits of glass we gathered up
To make us peeping shows;
We laid wild flowers behind and lapped
Them up in paper white,
And wonder thus in mystery wrapped
Claimed pins to see the sight.

Our little gardens there we made
Of blossoms all a-row,

And though they had no roots at all
We hoped to see them grow;
And in the cart-rut after showers
Of sudden summer rain
We filled our tiny water pots
And cherished them in vain.

We pulled the moss from apple trees
And gathered bits of straws
When weary twirling of our tops
And shooting of our taws;
We made birds' nests and thought that birds
Would like them ready-made,
And went full twenty times a day
To see if eggs were laid.

The long and swaily willow row
Where we for whips would climb,
How sweet their shadows used to grow
In merry harvest time;
We pulled boughs down and made a swee,
Snug hid from toil and sun,
And up we tossed right merrily
Till weary with the fun.

On summer eves with wild delight
We bawled the bat to spy
Who in the 'I spy' dusky light
Shrieked loud and flickered by,
And up we tossed our shuttlecocks
And tried to hit the moon
And wondered bats should fly so long
And they come down so soon.

We sought for nuts in secret nook
We thought none else could find,
And listened to the laughing brook
And mocked the singing wind;
We gathered acorns ripe and brown
That hung too high to pull,
Which friendly winds would shake a-down
Till all had pockets full.

Then loading home at day's decline
Each sought his corner stool,
Then went to bed till morning came
And crept again to school.
Yet there by pleasure unforsook
In nature's happy moods
The cuts in Fenning's Spelling Book
Made up for fields and woods.

Each noise that breathed around us then
Was magic all and song,
Wherever pastime found us then
Joy never led us wrong.
The wild bee in the blossom hung,
The coy bird's startled call
To find its home in danger—there
Was music in them all.

And o'er the first bumbarrel's nest
We wondered at the spell—
That birds who served no prenticeship
Could build their nests so well.
And finding linnet's moss was green
And finches choosing grey

And every finch's nest alike,
Our wits was all away.

Then blackbirds lining theirs with grass
And thrushes theirs with dung,
So for our lives we could not tell
From whence the wisdom sprung.
We marvelled much how little birds
Should ever be so wise,
And so we guessed some angel came
To teach them from the skies.

In winter too we traced the fields
And still felt summer joys;
We sought our hips and felt no cold—
Cold never came to boys—
The sloes appeared as choice as plums
When bitten by the frost
And crabs grew honey in the mouth
When apple time was past.

We rolled in sunshine lumps of snow
And called them mighty men,
And tired of pelting Bonaparte
We ran to slide again,
And ponds for glibbest ice were sought
With shouting and delight,
And tasks of spelling all were left
To get by heart at night.

And when it came—and round the fire
We sat—what joy was there:
The kitten dancing round the cork
That dangled from a chair

While we our scraps of paper burnt
To watch the flitting sparks,
And collect books were often torn
For parsons and for clerks.

Nought seemed too hard for us to do
But the sums upon our slates;
Nought seemed too hard for us to win
But the master's chair of state.
The 'Town of Troy' we tried and made
When our sums we could not try,
While we envied e'en the sparrow's wings
From our prison house to fly.

When twelve o'clock was counted out
The joy and strife began,
The shut of books, the hearty shout
As out of doors we ran.
Sunshine and showers who could withstand,
Our food and rapture they;
We took our dinner in our hands
To lose no time in play.

The morn when first we went to school,
Who can forget the morn?—
When the birch-whip lay upon the clock
And our hornbook it was torn.
We tore the little pictures out,
Less fond of books than play,
And only took one letter home
And that the letter 'A.'

I love in childhood's little book
To read its lessons through,

And o'er each pictured page to look
Because they read so true;
And there my heart creates anew
Love for each trifling thing
—Who can disdain the meanest weed
That shows its face in spring?

The daisy looks up in my face
As long ago it smiled;
It knows no change, but keeps its place
And takes me for a child.
The chaffinch in the hedgerow thorn
Cries 'pink pink pink' to hear
My footsteps in the early morn
As though a boy was near.

I seek no more the finch's nest,
Nor stoop for daisy flowers;
I grow a stranger to myself
In these delightful hours,
Yet when I hear the voice of spring
I can but call to mind
The pleasures which they used to bring,
The joys I used to find.

The firetail on the orchard wall
Keeps at its startled cry
Of 'tweet tut tut,' nor sees the morn
Of boyhood's mischief by;
It knows no change of changing time
By sickness never stung,
It feeds on hope's eternal prime
Around its brooded young.

Ponds where we played at 'Duck and Drake',
Where the ash with ivy grew,
Where we robbed the owl of all her eggs
And mocked her as she flew;
The broad tree in the spinney hedge
'Neath which the gypsies lay,
Where we our fine oak apples got
On the twenty-ninth of May:

These all remain as then they were
And are not changed a day,
And the ivy's crown's as near to green
As mine is to the grey;
It shades the pond, o'er hangs the stile;
And the oak is in the glen—
But the paths of joy are so worn out,
I can't find one again.

The merry wind still sings the song
As if no change had been,
The birds build nests the summer long,
The trees look full as green
As e'er they did in childhood's joy,
Though that hath long been by
When I a happy roving boy
In the fields had used to lie.

To tend the restless roving sheep
Or lead the quiet cow,
Toils that seemed more than slavery then—
How more than freedom now
Could we but feel as then we did
When joy too fond to fly

Would flutter round as soon as bid
And drive all troubles by.

But rainbows on an April cloud
And blossoms plucked in May
And painted eves that summer brings
Fade not so fast away,
Though grass is green, though flowers are gay,
And everywhere they be
What are the leaves on branches hung
Unto the withered tree?

Life's happiest gifts—and what are they?
Pearls by the morning strung
Which ere the noon are swept away;
Short as a cuckoo's song,
A nightingale's, the summer is.
Can pleasure make us proud
To think when swallows fly away
They leave her in her shroud?

Youth revels at his rising hour
With more than summer joys,
And rapture holds the fairy flower
Which reason soon destroys.
O sweet the bliss which fancy feigns
To hide the eyes of truth,
And beauteous still the charm remains
Of faces loved in youth.

And spring returns the blooming year
Just as it used to be,
And joys in youthful smiles appear

To mock the change in me.
Each night leaves memory ill at ease
And stirs an aching bosom
To think that seasons sweet as these
With me are out of blossom.

The fairest summer sinks in shade,
The sweetest blossom dies,
And age finds every beauty fade
That youth esteemed a prize.
The play breaks up, the blossom fades
And childhood disappears;
For higher dooms ambition aims
And care grows into years.

But time we often blame him wrong,
That rude destroying time,
And follow him with sorrow's song
When he hath done no crime.
Our joys in youth are often sold
In folly's thoughtless fray,
And many feel their hearts grow old
Before their heads are grey.

The past—there lies in that one word
Joys more than wealth can crown,
Nor could a million call them back
Though muses wrote them down;
The sweetest joys imagined yet,
The beauties that surpassed
All life or fancy ever met
Are there among the past.

The Moorhen's Nest

O poesy's power, thou overpowering sweet
That renders hearts that love thee all unmeet
For this rude world its trouble and its care,
Loading the heart with joys it cannot bear
That warms and chills and burns and bursts at last
O'er broken hopes and troubles never past,
I pay thee worship at a rustic shrine
And dream o'er joys I still imagine mine;
I pick up flowers and pebbles and by thee
As gems and jewels they appear to me;
I pick out pictures round the fields that lie
In my mind's heart like things that cannot die,
Like picking hopes and making friends with all.
Yet glass will often bear a harder fall:
As bursting bottles lose the precious wine,
Hope's casket breaks and I the gems resign;
Pain shadows on till feeling's self decays
And all such pleasures leave me is their praise.
And thus each fairy vision melts away
Like evening landscapes from the face of day,
Till hope returns with April's dewy reign,
And then I start and seek for joys again
And pick her fragments up to herd anew
Like fairy-riches pleasure loves to view,

And these associations of the past
Like summer pictures in a winter blast
Renews my heart to feelings as the rain
Falls on the earth and bids it thrive again.
Then e'en the fallow fields appear so fair,
The very weeds make sweetest gardens there
And summer there puts garments on so gay
I hate the plough that comes to disarray
Her holiday delights—and labour's toil
Seems vulgar curses on the sunny soil
And man the only object that distrains
Earth's garden into deserts for his gains.
Leave him his schemes of gain—'tis wealth to me
Wild heaths to trace, and note their broken tree
Which lightning shivered and which nature tries
To keep alive for poesy to prize,
Upon whose mossy roots my leisure sits
To hear the birds pipe o'er their amorous fits,
Though less beloved for singing than the taste
They have to choose such homes upon the waste—
Rich architects!—and then the spots to see
How picturesque their dwellings make them be:
The wild romances of the poet's mind
No sweeter pictures for their tales can find.
And so I glad my heart and rove along,
Now finding nests, then listening to a song,
Then drinking fragrance whose perfuming cheats
Tinges life's sours and bitters into sweets,
That heart-stirred fragrance when the summer rain
Lays the road dust and sprouts the grass again,
Filling the cracks up on the beaten paths
And breathing incense from the mower's swaths,

Incense the bards and prophets of old days
Met in the wilderness to glad their praise;
And in these summer walks I seem to feel
These bible-pictures in their essence steal
Around me—and the ancientness of joy
Breathe from the woods till pleasures even cloy,
Yet holy-breathing manna seemly falls
With angel answers if a trouble calls.
And then I walk and swing my stick for joy
And catch at little pictures passing by:
A gate whose posts are two old dotterel trees,
A close with molehills sprinkled o'er its leas,
A little footbrig with its crossing rail,
A wood-gap stopped with ivy-wreathing pale,
A crooked stile each path-crossed spinney owns,
A brooklet forded by its stepping stones,
A wood-bank mined with rabbit holes—and then
An old oak leaning o'er a badger's den
Whose cave-mouth enters 'neath the twisted charms
Of its old roots and keeps it safe from harms,
Pickaxes, spades, and all its strength confounds
When hunted foxes hide from chasing hounds.
Then comes the meadows where I love to see
A flood-washed bank support an aged tree
Whose roots are bare, yet some with foothold good
Crankle and spread and strike beneath the flood,
Yet still it leans, as safer hold to win
On t'other side, and seems as tumbling in,
While every summer finds it green and gay
And winter leaves it safe as did the may.
Nor does the moorhen find its safety vain,
For on its roots their last year's homes remain,

And once again a couple from the brood
Seek their old birthplace and in safety's mood
Lodge there their flags and lay—though danger comes,
It dares and tries and cannot reach their homes—
And so they hatch their eggs and sweetly dream
On their shelfed nests that bridge the gulfy stream,
And soon the sooty brood from fear elopes
Where bulrush forests give them sweeter hopes,
Their hanging nest that aids their wishes well
Each leaves for water as it leaves the shell,
And dive and dare and every gambol try
Till they themselves to other scenes can fly.

The Progress of Rhyme

O soul-enchanting poesy,
Thou'st long been all the world with me:
When poor thy presence grows my wealth,
When sick thy visions gives me health,
When sad thy sunny smile is joy
And was from e'en a tiny boy,
When trouble was and toiling care
Seemed almost more than I could bear,
While threshing in the dusty barn
Or squashing in the ditch to earn
A pittance that would scarce allow
One joy to smooth my sweating brow
Where drop by drop would chase and fall—
Thy presence triumphed over all.
The vulgar they might frown and sneer,
Insult was mean but never near:
'Twas poesy's self that stopped the sigh
And malice met with no reply.
So was it in my earlier day
When sheep to corn had strayed away
Or horses closen gaps had broke
Ere suns had peeped or I awoke:
My master's frowns might force the tear
But poesy came to check and cheer—

It glistened in my shamèd eye
But ere it fell the swoof was by—
I thought of luck in future days
When even he might find a praise.
I looked on poesy like a friend
To cheer me till my life should end:
'Twas like a parent's first regard
And love when beauty's voice was heard,
'Twas joy, 'twas hope and maybe fear,
But still 'twas rapture everywhere—
My heart were ice unmoved to dwell
Nor care for one I loved so well
Through rough and smooth, through good and ill—
That led me and attends me still.
It was an early joy to me
That joy was love and poesy
And but for thee my idle lay
Had ne'er been urged in early day,
The harp imagination strung
Had ne'er been dreamed of—but among
The flowers in summer's fields of joy
I'd lain an idle rustic boy,
No hope to think of, fear or care,
And even love a stranger there—
But poesy that vision flung
Around me as I hummed or sung;
I glowered on beauty passing by
Yet hardly turned my sheepish eye;
I worshipped, yet could hardly dare
To show I knew the goddess there
Lest my presumptuous stare should gain
But frowns, ill humour and disdain.

My first ambition was its praise,
My struggles aye in early days.
Had I by vulgar boldness torn
That hope when it was newly born,
By rudeness, gibes and vulgar tongue,
The curse of the unfeeling throng,
Their scorn had frowned upon the lay
And hope and song had died away,
And I with nothing to atone
Had felt myself indeed alone.
But promises of days to come
The very fields would seem to hum,
Those burning days when I should dare
To sing aloud my worship there,
When beauty's self might turn its eye
Of praise—what could I do but try?
'Twas winter then, but summer shone
From heaven when I was all alone;
And summer came and every weed
Of great or little had its meed;
Without its leaves there wa'n't a bower
Nor one poor weed without its flower—
'Twas love and pleasure all along.
I felt that I'd a right to song
And sung—but in a timid strain
Of fondness for my native plain;
For everything I felt a love,
The weeds below, the birds above,
And weeds that bloomed in summer's hours,
I thought they should be reckoned flowers;
They made a garden free for all
And so I loved them great and small

And sung of some that pleased my eye,
Nor could I pass the thistle by
But paused and thought it could not be
A weed in nature's poesy.
No matter for protecting wall,
No matter though they chance to fall
Where sheep and cows and oxen lie,
The kindly rain when they're a-dry
Falls on them with as plenteous showers
As when it waters garden flowers—
They look up with a blushing eye
Upon a tender watching sky
And still enjoy the kindling smile
Of sunshine, though they live with toil,
As garden flowers with all their care,
For nature's love is even there.
And so it cheered me while I lay
Among their beautiful array
To think that I in humble dress
Might have a right to happiness
And sing as well as greater men,
And then I strung the lyre again
And heartened up o'er toil and fear
And lived with rapture everywhere
Till dayshine to my themes did come.
Just as a blossom bursts to bloom
And finds itself in thorny ways,
So did my musings meet with praise,
And though no garden care had I
My heart had love for poesy,
A simple love, a wild esteem,
As heartfelt as the linnet's dream

That mutters in its sleep at night
Some notes from ecstasy's delight—
Thus did I dream o'er joys and lie
Muttering dream-songs of poesy.
The night dislimned and waking day
Shook from wood leaves the drops away;
Hope came, storms calmed, and hue and cry
With her false pictures herded by,
With tales of help when help was not,
Of friends who urged to write or blot,
Whose taste were such that mine were shame
Had they not helped it into fame.
Poh! let the idle rumour ill,
Their vanity is never still—
My harp though simple was my own.
When I was in the fields alone
With none to help and none to hear,
To bid me either hope or fear,
The bird or bee its chords would sound,
The air hummed melodies around,
I caught with eager ear the strain
And sung the music o'er again.
Or love or instinct flowing strong,
Fields were the essence of the song
And fields and woods are still as mine,
Real teachers that are all divine.
So if my song be weak or tame
'Tis I not they who bear the blame,
But hope and cheer, through good and ill
They are my aids to worship still,
Still growing on a gentle tide
Nor foes could mar nor friends could guide.

Like pasture brooks through sun and shade,
Crooked as channels chance hath made,
It rambles as it loves to stray
And hope and feeling leads the way.
Ay, birds, no matter what the tune
Or 'croak' or 'tweet', 'twas nature's boon
That brought them joy, and music flung
Its spell o'er every matin sung
And e'en the sparrow's chirp to me
Was song in its felicity.
When grief hung o'er me like a cloud
Till hope seemed even in her shroud,
I whispered poesy's spells till they
Gleamed round me like a summer's day;
When tempests o'er my labours sung,
My soul to its responses rung
And joined the chorus till the storm
Fell all unheeded, void of harm;
And each old leaning shielding tree
Were princely palaces to me
Where I could sit me down and chime
My unheard rhapsodies to rhyme.
All I beheld of grand, with time
Grew up to beautiful's sublime:
The arching groves of ancient limes
That into roofs like churches climb,
Grain intertwisting into grain
That stops the sun and stops the rain
And spreads a gloom that never smiles,
Like ancient halls and minster aisles,
While all without a beauteous screen
Of summer's luscious leaves is seen,

While heard that everlasting hum
Of insects haunting where they bloom,
As though 'twas nature's very place
Of worship where her mighty race
Of insect life and spirits too
In summer time were wont to go—
Both insects and the breath of flowers
To sing their maker's mighty powers.
I've thought so as I used to rove
Through Burghley Park, that darksome grove
Of limes where twilight lingered grey
Like evening in the midst of day,
And felt without a single skill
That instinct that would not be still
To think of song sublime beneath
That heaved my bosom like my breath,
That burned and chilled and went and came
Without or uttering or a name
Until the vision waked with time
And left me itching after rhyme.
Where little pictures idly tells
Of nature's powers and nature's spells,
I felt and shunned the idle vein,
Laid down the pen and toiled again,
But spite of all, through good and ill
It was and is my worship still.
No matter how the world approved,
'Twas nature listened—I that loved.
No matter how the lyre was strung,
From my own heart the music sprung.
The cowboy with his oaten straw,
Although he hardly heard or saw

No more of music than he made,
'Twas sweet—and when I plucked the blade
Of grass upon the woodland hill
To mock the birds with artless skill,
No music in the world beside
Seemed half so sweet—till mine was tried.
So my boy-worship, poesy,
Made e'en the muses pleased with me,
Until I even danced for joy,
A happy and a lonely boy,
Each object to my ear and eye
Made paradise of poesy.
I heard the blackbird in the dell
Sing sweet—could I but sing as well,
I thought, until the bird in glee
Seemed pleased and paused to answer me.
And nightingales—O I have stood
Beside the pingle and the wood
And o'er the old oak railing hung
To listen every note they sung,
And left boys making taws of clay
To muse and listen half the day.
The more I listened and the more
Each note seemed sweeter than before,
And aye so different was the strain
She'd scarce repeat the note again:
'Chew-chew chew-chew' and higher still,
'Cheer-cheer cheer-cheer' more loud and shrill,
'Cheer-up cheer-up cheer-up'—and dropped
Low—'Tweet tweet jug jug jug'—and stopped
One moment just to drink the sound
Her music made, and then a round

Of stranger witching notes was heard
As if it was a stranger bird:
'Wew-wew wew-wew chur-chur chur-chur
Woo-it woo-it'—could this be her?
'Tee-rew tee-rew tee-rew tee-rew
Chew-rit chew-rit'—and ever new—
'Will-will will-will grig-grig grig-grig.'
The boy stopped sudden on the brig
To hear the 'tweet tweet tweet' so shrill,
Then 'jug jug jug,' and all was still
A minute—when a wilder strain
Made boys and woods to pause again.
Words were not left to hum the spell.
Could they be birds that sung so well?
I thought, and maybe more than I,
That music's self had left the sky
To cheer me with its magic strain,
And then I hummed the words again
Till fancy pictured standing by
My heart's companion, poesy.

　　No friends had I to guide or aid
The struggles young ambition made.
In silent shame the harp was tried
And rapture's guess the tune applied,
Yet o'er the songs my parents sung
My ear in silent musings hung;
Their kindness wishes did regard,
They sung and joy was my reward.
All else was but a proud decree,
The right of bards and nought to me,
A title that I dare not claim
And hid it like a private shame.

I whispered aye and felt a fear
To speak aloud though none was near—
I dreaded laughter more than blame
And dare not sing aloud for shame,
So all unheeded, lone and free,
I felt it happiness to be
Unknown, obscure and like a tree
In woodland peace and privacy.
No, not a friend on earth had I
But my own kin and poesy,
Nor wealth—and yet I felt indeed
As rich as anybody need
To be—for health and hope and joy
Was mine although a lonely boy,
And what I felt—as now I sing—
Made friends of all and everything
Save man, the vulgar and the low.
The polished 'twas not mine to know
Who paid me in my after days
And gave me even more than praise:
'Twas then I found that friends indeed
Were needed when I'd less to need.
The pea that independent springs
When in its blossom trails and clings
To every help that lingers by,
And I when classed with poesy,
Who stood unbrunt the heaviest shower,
Felt feeble as that very flower
And helpless all—but beauty's smile
Is harvest for the hardest toil,
Whose smiles I little thought to win
With ragged coat and downy chin,

A clownish silent haynish boy
Who even felt ashamed of joy,
So dirty, ragged and so low,
With nought to recommend or show
That I was worthy e'en a smile
—Had I but felt amid my toil
That I in days to come should be
A little light in minstrelsy
And in the blush of after days
Win beauty's smile and beauty's praise,
My heart with lonely fancy warm
Had even bursted with the charm.
And one, ay one whose very name
I loved—whose look was even fame—
From rich delicious eyes of blue
In smiles and rapture ever new,
Her timid step, her fairy form,
Her face with blushes ever warm,
Praise did my rhyming feelings move—
I saw the blush and thought it love.
And all ambitious thee to please
My heart was ever ill at ease;
I saw thy beauty grow with days
And tried song-pictures in thy praise,
And all of fair or beautiful
Were thine akin—nor could I pull
The blossoms that I thought divine,
As hurting beauty like to thine.
So where they grew I let them be
And though I dare not look to thee
Of love—to them I talked aloud
And grew ambitious from the crowd

With hopes that I should one day be
Belovèd with the praise of thee.
But I mistook in early day
The world—and so our hopes decay.
Yet that same cheer in after toils
Was poesy—and still she smiles
As sweet as blossoms to the tree
And hope, love, joy, are poesy.

Remembrances

Summer pleasures they are gone, like to visions every one,
And the cloudy days of autumn and of winter cometh on:
I tried to call them back, but unbidden they are gone
Far away from heart and eye and for ever far away,
Dear heart, and can it be that such raptures meet decay?
I thought them all eternal when by Langley Bush I lay;
I thought them joys eternal when I used to shout and play
On its bank at 'clink and bandy', 'chock' and 'taw' and
    ducking-stone,
Where silence sitteth now on the wild heath as her own
Like a ruin of the past all alone.

When I used to lie and sing by old Eastwell's boiling spring,
When I used to tie the willow boughs together for a 'swing'
And fish with crooked pins and thread and never catch a thing,
With heart just like a feather—now as heavy as a stone.
When beneath old Lea Close Oak I the bottom branches broke
To make our harvest cart, like so many working folk,
And then to cut a straw at the brook to have a soak,
O I never dreamed of parting or that trouble had a sting
Or that pleasures like a flock of birds would ever take to wing,
Leaving nothing but a little naked spring.

When jumping time away on old Crossberry Way
And eating 'awes like sugar-plums ere they had lost the may,

And skipping like a leveret before the peep of day
On the roly-poly up and downs of pleasant Swordy Well,
When in Round Oak's narrow lane as the south got black again
We sought the hollow ash that was shelter from the rain
With our pockets full of peas we had stolen from the grain,
How delicious was the dinner time on such a showery day—
O words are poor receipts for what time hath stole away,
The ancient pulpit trees and the play.

When for school o'er 'Little Field' with its brook and wooden brig
Where I swaggered like a man though I was not half so big,
While I held my little plough though 'twas but a willow twig,
And drove my team along made of nothing but a name—
'Gee hep' and 'hoit' and 'woi'—O I never call to mind
Those pleasant names of places but I leave a sigh behind,
While I see the little mouldywarps hang sweeing to the wind
On the only aged willow that in all the field remains,
And nature hides her face while they're sweeing in their chains
And in a silent murmuring complains.

Here was commons for their hills where they seek for freedom still,
Though every common's gone and though traps are set to kill
The little homeless miners—O it turns my bosom chill
When I think of old 'Sneap Green', Paddock's Nook and Hilly Snow
Where bramble bushes grew and the daisy gemmed in dew
And the hills of silken grass like to cushions to the view,
Where we threw the pismire crumbs when we'd nothing else to do—
All levelled like a desert by the never-weary plough,
All banished like the sun where that cloud is passing now,
And settled here for ever on its brow.

O I never thought that joys would run away from boys
Or that boys should change their minds and forsake such summer joys,

But alack I never dreamed that the world had other toys
To petrify first feelings like the fable into stone,
Till I found the pleasure past and a winter come at last—
Then the fields were sudden bare and the sky got overcast
And boyhood's pleasing haunts like a blossom in the blast
Was shrivelled to a withered weed and trampled down and done,
Till vanished was the morning spring and set the summer sun
And winter fought her battle-strife and won.

By Langley Bush I roam, but the bush hath left its hill;
On Cowper Green I stray, 'tis a desert strange and chill;
And spreading Lea Close Oak, ere decay had penned its will,
To the axe of the spoiler and self-interest fell a prey;
And Crossberry Way and old Round Oak's narrow lane
With its hollow trees like pulpits, I shall never see again:
Enclosure like a Bonaparte let not a thing remain,
It levelled every bush and tree and levelled every hill
And hung the moles for traitors—though the brook is running still,
It runs a naked stream, cold and chill.

O had I known as then joy had left the paths of men,
I had watched her night and day, be sure, and never slept again,
And when she turned to go, O I'd caught her mantle then
And wooed her like a lover by my lonely side to stay,
Ay, knelt and worshipped on as love in beauty's bower,
And clung upon her smiles as a bee upon a flower,
And gave her heart my poesies all cropped in a sunny hour
As keepsakes and pledges all to never fade away—
But love never heeded to treasure up the may,
So it went the common road with decay.

Swordy Well

I've loved thee, Swordy Well, and love thee still:
Long was I with thee, tenting sheep and cow
In boyhood, ramping up each steepy hill
To play at 'roly poly' down—and now
A man I trifle o'er thee, cares to kill,
Haunting thy mossy steeps to botanise
And hunt the orchis tribes where nature's skill
Doth like my thoughts run into fantasies—
Spider and bee all mimicking at will,
Displaying powers that fools the proudly wise,
Showing the wonders of great nature's plan
In trifles insignificant and small,
Puzzling the power of that great trifle man,
Who finds no reason to be proud at all.

Emmonsails Heath in Winter

I love to see the old heath's withered brake
Mingle its crimpled leaves with furze and ling
While the old heron from the lonely lake
Starts slow and flaps his melancholy wing
And oddling crow in idle motions swing
On the half-rotten ash tree's topmost twig
Beside whose trunk the gypsy makes his bed—
Up flies the bouncing woodcock from the brig
Where a black quagmire quakes beneath the tread;
The fieldfare chatters in the whistling thorn
And for the 'awe round fields and closen rove,
And coy bumbarrels twenty in a drove
Flit down the hedgerows in the frozen plain
And hang on little twigs and start again.

Love and Memory

Thou art gone the dark journey
That leaves no returning;
'Tis fruitless to mourn thee
But who can help mourning
To think of the life
That did laugh on thy brow
In the beautiful past
Left so desolate now?

When youth seemed immortal,
So sweet did it weave
Heaven's halo around thee
Earth's hopes to deceive;
Thou fairest and dearest
Where many were fair,
To my heart thou art nearest
Though this name is but there.

The nearer the fountain
More pure the stream flows
And sweeter to fancy
The bud of the rose,
And now thou'rt in heaven
More pure is the birth
Of thoughts that wake of thee
Than aught upon earth.

As a bud green in spring,
As a rose blown in June,
Thy beauty looked out
And departed as soon;
Heaven saw thee too fair
For earth's tenants of clay
And ere age did thee wrong
Thou wert summoned away.

I know thou art happy,
Why in grief need I be?
Yet I am and the more so
To feel it's for thee,
For thy presence possessed
As thy absence destroyed
The most that I loved
And the all I enjoyed.

So I try to seek pleasure
But vainly I try
Now joy's cup is drained
And hope's fountain is dry;
I mix with the living,
Yet what do I see?
Only more cause for sorrow
In losing of thee.

The year has its winter
As well as its May,
So the sweetest must leave us
And the fairest decay;
Suns leave us tonight
And their light none may borrow,

So joy retreats from us
Overtaken by sorrow.

The sun greets the spring
And the blossom the bee,
The grass the blea hill
And the leaf the bare tree,
But suns nor yet seasons
As sweet as they be
Shall ever more greet me
With tidings of thee.

The voice of the cuckoo
Is merry at noon
And the song of the nightingale
Gladdens the moon,
But the gayest today
May be saddest tomorrow
And the loudest in joy
Sink the deepest in sorrow.

For the lovely in death
And the fairest must die,
Fall once and for ever
Like stars from the sky;
So in vain do I mourn thee,
I know it's in vain,
Who would wish thee from joy
To earth's troubles again?

Yet thy love shed upon me
Life more than mine own,
And now thou art from me

My being is gone;
Words know not my grief
Thus without thee to dwell,
Yet in one I felt all
When life bade thee farewell.

The Fallen Elm

Old elm that murmured in our chimney top
The sweetest anthem autumn ever made
And into mellow whispering calms would drop
When showers fell on thy many-coloured shade
And when dark tempests mimic thunder made
While darkness came as it would strangle light
With the black tempest of a winter night
That rocked thee like a cradle to thy root,
How did I love to hear the winds upbraid
Thy strength without—while all within was mute.
It seasoned comfort to our hearts' desire,
We felt thy kind protection like a friend
And edged our chairs up closer to the fire,
Enjoying comforts that was never penned.
Old favourite tree, thou'st seen times changes lower,
Though change till now did never injure thee,
For time beheld thee as her sacred dower
And nature claimed thee her domestic tree;
Storms came and shook thee many a weary hour,
Yet steadfast to thy home thy roots hath been;
Summers of thirst parched round thy homely bower
Till earth grew iron—still thy leaves was green.
The childern sought thee in thy summer shade
And made their playhouse rings of sticks and stone;

The mavis sang and felt himself alone
While in thy leaves his early nest was made
And I did feel his happiness mine own,
Nought heeding that our friendship was betrayed—
Friend not inanimate, though stocks and stones
There are and many formed of flesh and bones,
Thou owned a language by which hearts are stirred
Deeper than by a feeling clothed in words,
And speakest now what's known of every tongue,
Language of pity and the force of wrong.
What cant assumes, what hypocrites will dare,
Speaks home to truth and shows it what they are.
I see a picture which thy fate displays
And learn a lesson from thy destiny:
Self-interest saw thee stand in freedom's ways,
So thy old shadow must a tyrant be;
Thou'st heard the knave abusing those in power,
Bawl freedom loud and then oppress the free;
Thou'st sheltered hypocrites in many a shower
That when in power would never shelter thee;
Thou'st heard the knave supply his canting powers
With wrong's illusions when he wanted friends,
That bawled for shelter when he lived in showers
And when clouds vanished made thy shade amends—
With axe at root he felled thee to the ground
And barked of freedom. O I hate the sound!
Time hears its visions speak and age sublime
Had made thee a disciple unto time.
It grows the cant term of enslaving tools
To wrong another by the name of right;
It grows the licence of o'erbearing fools
To cheat plain honesty by force of might.

Thus came enclosure—ruin was its guide
But freedom's clapping hands enjoyed the sight
Though comfort's cottage soon was thrust aside
And workhouse prisons raised upon the site.
E'en nature's dwellings far away from men—
The common heath—became the spoilers' prey:
The rabbit had not where to make his den
And labour's only cow was drove away.
No matter—wrong was right and right was wrong
And freedom's bawl was sanction to the song.
—Such was thy ruin, music-making elm:
The rights of freedom was to injure thine.
As thou wert served, so would they overwhelm
In freedom's name the little that is mine.
And there are knaves that brawl for better laws
And cant of tyranny in stronger powers,
Who glut their vile unsatiated maws
And freedom's birthright from the weak devours.

The Landrail

How sweet and pleasant grows the way
Through summer time again,
While landrails call from day to day
Amid the grass and grain.

We hear it in the weeding time
When knee-deep waves the corn,
We hear it in the summer's prime
Through meadows, night and morn;

And now I hear it in the grass
That grows as sweet again,
And let a minute's notice pass
And now 'tis in the grain.

'Tis like a fancy everywhere,
A sort of living doubt,
We know 'tis something but it ne'er
Will blab the secret out.

If heard in close or meadow plots
It flies if we pursue,
But follows if we notice not
The close and meadow through.

Boys know the note of many a bird
In their bird-nesting rounds,
But when the landrail's noise is heard
They wonder at the sounds;

They look in every tuft of grass
That's in their rambles met,
They peep in every bush they pass
And none the wiser yet,

And still they hear the craiking sound
And still they wonder why—
It surely can't be underground
Nor is it in the sky,

And yet 'tis heard in every vale,
An undiscovered song,
And makes a pleasant wonder tale
For all the summer long.

The shepherd whistles through his hands
And starts with many a whoop
His busy dog across the lands
In hopes to fright it up.

'Tis still a minute's length or more
Till dogs are off and gone,
Then sings and louder than before
But keeps the secret on.

Yet accident will often meet
The nest within its way,

And weeders when they weed the wheat
Discover where they lay,

And mowers on the meadow lea
Chance on their noisy guest
And wonder what the bird can be
That lays without a nest.

In simple holes that birds will rake
When dusting in the ground;
They drop their eggs of curious make,
Deep-blotched and nearly round—

A mystery still to men and boys
Who knows not where they lay
And guess it but a summer noise
Among the meadow-hay.

Pastoral Poesy

True poesy is not in words
But images that thoughts express
By which the simplest hearts are stirred
To elevated happiness;

Mere books would be but useless things
Where none had taste or mind to read,
Like unknown lands where beauty springs
And none are there to heed;

But poesy is a language meet
And fields are everyone's employ—
The wild flower 'neath the shepherd's feet
Looks up and gives him joy—

A language that is ever green,
That feelings unto all impart,
As 'awthorn blossoms soon as seen
Give May to every heart.

The pictures that our summer minds
In summer's dwellings meet,
The fancies that the shepherd finds
To make his leisure sweet,

The dustmills that the cowboy delves
In banks for dust to run,
Creates a summer in ourselves—
He does as we have done—

An image to the mind is brought
Where happiness enjoys
An easy thoughtlessness of thought
And meets excess of joys;

The world is in that little spot
With him—and all beside
Is nothing, all a life forgot
In feelings satisfied:

And such is poesy its power
May varied lights employ,
Yet to all mind it gives the dower
Of self-creating joy;

And whether it be hill or moor,
I feel where'er I go
A silence that discourses more
Than any tongue can do,

Unruffled quietness hath made
A peace in every place
And woods are resting in their shade
Of social loneliness;

The storm from which the shepherd turns
To pull his beaver down

While he upon the heath sojourns
Which autumn bleaches brown

Is music aye, and more indeed
To those of musing mind
Who through the yellow woods proceed
And listen to the wind.

The poet in his fitful glee
And fancy's many moods
Meets it as some strange melody
And poem of the woods;

It sings and whistles in his mind
And then it talks aloud
While by some leaning tree reclined
He shuns a coming cloud

That sails its bulk against the sun,
A mountain in the light,
He heeds not for the storm begun
But dallies with delight,

And now a harp that flings around
The music of the wind
The poet often hears the sound
When beauty fills the mind.

The morn with safforn strips and grey
Or blushing to the view,
Like summer fields when run away
In weeds of crimson hue,

Will simple shepherds' hearts imbue
With nature's poesy,
Who inly fancy while they view
How grand must heaven be.

With every musing mind she steals
Attendance on their way,
The simplest thing her heart reveals
Is seldom thrown away.

The old man full of leisure hours
Sits cutting at his door
Rude fancy sticks to tie his flowers
—They're sticks and nothing more

With many passing by his door—
But pleasure has its bent:
With him 'tis happiness and more,
Heart-satisfied content.

Those box-edged borders that impart
Their fragrance near his door
Hath been the comfort of his heart
For sixty years and more;

That mossy thatch above his head
In winter's drifting showers
To him and his old partner made
A music many hours;

It patted to their hearts a joy
That humble comfort made,

A little fire to keep them dry
And shelter overhead;

And such, no matter what they call
Each, all are nothing less
Than poesy's power that gives to all
A cheerful blessedness.

So would I my own mind employ
And my own heart impress
That poesy's self's a dwelling joy
Of humble quietness;

So would I for the biding joy
That to such thoughts belong
That I life's errand may employ
As harmless as a song.

The Wren

Why is the cuckoo's melody preferred
And nightingale's rich song so fondly praised
In poet's rhymes? Is there no other bird
Of nature's minstrelsy that oft hath raised
One's heart to ecstasy and mirth as well?
I judge not how another's taste is caught—
With mine there's other birds that bear the bell,
Whose song hath crowds of happy memories brought,
Such the wood robin singing in the dell
And little wren that many a time hath sought
Shelter from showers in huts where I did dwell
In early spring, the tenant of the plain
Tenting my sheep, and still they come to tell
The happy stories of the past again.

Wood Pictures in Spring

The rich brown-umber hue the oaks unfold
When spring's young sunshine bathes their trunks in gold,
So rich, so beautiful, so past the power
Of words to paint—my heart aches for the dower
The pencil gives to soften and infuse
This brown luxuriance of unfolding hues,
This living luscious tinting woodlands give
Into a landscape that might breathe and live,
And this old gate that claps against the tree
The entrance of spring's paradise should be—
Yet paint itself with living nature fails:
The sunshine threading through these broken rails
In mellow shades no pencil e'er conveys,
And mind alone feels fancies and portrays.

The Hollow Tree

How oft a summer shower hath started me
To seek for shelter in an hollow tree:
Old huge ash-dotterel wasted to a shell,
Whose vigorous head still grew and flourished well,
Where ten might sit upon the battered floor
And still look round discovering room for more,
And he who chose a hermit life to share
Might have a door and make a cabin there—
They seemed so like a house that our desires
Would call them so and make our gypsy fires
And eat field dinners of the juicy peas
Till we were wet and drabbled to the knees.
But in our old tree house, rain as it might,
Not one drop fell although it rained till night.

The Sand Martin

Thou hermit haunter of the lonely glen
And common wild and heath—the desolate face
Of rude waste landscapes far away from men
Where frequent quarries give thee dwelling place,
With strangest taste and labour undeterred
Drilling small holes along the quarry's side,
More like the haunts of vermin than a bird
And seldom by the nesting boy descried—
I've seen thee far away from all thy tribe
Flirting about the unfrequented sky
And felt a feeling that I can't describe
Of lone seclusion and a hermit joy
To see thee circle round nor go beyond
That lone heath and its melancholy pond.

from
The Rural Muse
(1835)

from To the Rural Muse

'Smile on my verse and look the world to love'

Muse of the fields, oft have I said farewell
To thee, my boon companion loved so long,
And hung thy sweet harp in the bushy dell
For abler hands to wake an abler song.
Much did I fear my homage did thee wrong,
Yet, loath to leave, as oft I turned again
And to its wires mine idle hands would cling,
Torturing it into song. It may be vain,
Yet still I try, ere fancy droops her wing
And hopeless silence comes to numb its every string.

Muse of the pasture brooks, on thy calm sea
Of poesy I've sailed, and though the will
To speed were greater than my prowess be,
I've ventured with much fear of usage ill,
Yet more of joy. Though timid be my skill,
As not to dare the depths of mightier streams,
Yet rocks abide in shallow ways and I
Have much of fear to mingle with my dreams.
Yet, lovely muse, I still believe thee by
And think I see thee smile and so forget I sigh.

Muse of the cottage hearth, oft did I tell
My hopes to thee, nor feared to plead in vain,

But felt around my heart thy witching spell
That bade me as thy worshipper remain:
I did so, and still worship. Oh once again
Smile on my offerings and so keep them green,
Bedeck my fancies like the clouds of even,
Mingling all hues which thou from heaven dost glean!
To me a portion of thy power be given,
If theme so mean as mine may merit aught of heaven.

For thee in youth I culled the simple flower
That on thy bosom gained a sweeter hue,
And took thy hand along life's sunny hour,
Meeting the sweetest joys that ever grew;
More friends were needless and my foes were few,
Though freedom then be deemed as rudeness now
And what once won thy praise now meet disdain,
Yet the last wreath I braided for thy brow
Thy smiles did so commend, it made me vain
To weave another one and hope for praise again.

With thee the spirit of departed years
Wakes that sweet voice which time hath rendered dumb
And freshens, like to spring, loves, hopes and fears
That in my bosom found an early home,
Wooing the heart to ecstasy. I come
To thee when sick of care, of joy bereft,
Seeking the pleasures that are found in bloom
And happy hopes that time hath only left
Around the haunts where thou didst erst sojourn,
Then smile, sweet cherubim, and welcome my return.

With thee the raptures of life's early day
Appear, and all that pleased me when a boy.

Though pains and cares have torn the best away
And winters crept between us to destroy,
Do thou commend, the recompense is joy:
The tempest of the heart shall soon be calm.
Though sterner truth against my dreams rebel,
Hope feels success; and all my spirits warm
To strike with happier mood thy simple shell
And seize thy mantle's hem—O say not fare-thee-well.

Still, sweet enchantress, youth's strong feelings move
That from thy presence their existence took:
The innocent idolatry and love,
Paying thee worship in each secret nook,
That fancied friends in tree and flower and brook,
Shaped clouds to angels and beheld them smile
And heard commending tongues in every wind.
Life's grosser fancies did these dreams defile,
Yet not entirely root them from the mind;
I think I hear them still and often look behind.

Ay, I have heard thee in the summer wind,
As if commending what I sung to thee;
Ay, I have seen thee on a cloud reclined,
Kindling my fancies into poesy;
I saw thee smile and took the praise to me.
In beauties past all beauty thou wert drest;
I thought the very clouds around thee knelt;
I saw the sun to linger in the west,
Paying thee worship; and as eve did melt
In dews, they seemed thy tears for sorrows I had felt.

Sweeter than flowers on beauty's bosom hung,
Sweeter than dreams of happiness above,

Sweeter than themes by lips of beauty sung,
Are the young fancies of a poet's love
When round his thoughts thy trancing visions move
In floating melody no notes may sound;
The world is all forgot and past his care,
While on thy harp thy fingers lightly bound,
As winning him its melody to share,
And heaven itself, with him, where is it then but there?

. . . .

Autumn

Siren of sullen moods and fading hues,
Yet haply not incapable of joy,
Sweet autumn, I thee hail
With welcome all unfeigned,
And oft as morning from her lattice peeps
To beckon up the sun, I seek with thee
To drink the dewy breath
Of fields left fragrant then,

In solitudes where no frequented paths
But what thy own foot makes betray thine home,
Stealing obtrusive there
To meditate thy end
By overshadowed ponds in woody nooks
With ramping sallows lined and crowding sedge
Which woo the winds to play
And with them dance for joy,

And meadow pools torn wide by lawless floods
Where water lilies spread their oily leaves
On which, as wont, the fly
Oft battens in the sun;
Where leans the mossy willow half-way o'er,
On which the shepherd crawls astride to throw
His angle clear of weeds
That crowd the water's brim;

Or crispy hills and hollows scant of sward,
Where step by step the patient lonely boy
Hath cut rude flights of stairs
To climb their steepy sides;
Then tracking at their feet, grown hoarse with noise,
The crawling brook that ekes its weary speed
And struggles through the weeds
With faint and sullen brawl—

These haunts I long have favoured, more as now
With thee thus wandering, moralising on,
Stealing glad thoughts from grief,
And happy though I sigh.
Sweet vision, with the wild dishevelled hair
And raiment shadowy of each wind's embrace,
Fain would I win thine harp
To one accordant theme;

Now not inaptly craved, communing thus
Beneath the curdled arms of this stunt oak,
We pillow on the grass
And fondly ruminate
O'er the disordered scenes of woods and fields,
Ploughed lands thin-travelled with half-hungry sheep,
Pastures tracked deep with cows,
Where small birds seek for seed;

Marking the cowboy that so merry trills
His frequent unpremeditated song,
Wooing the winds to pause
Till echo brawls again
As on with plashy step and clouted shoon
He roves half-indolent and self-employed

To rob the little birds
Of hips and pendant haws

And sloes dim covered as with dewy veils
And rambling bramble-berries, pulp and sweet,
Arching their prickly trails
Half o'er the narrow lane;
Noting the hedger front with stubborn face
The dank blea wind that whistles thinly by
His leathern garb thorn-proof
And cheek red-hot with toil.

And o'er the pleachy lands of mellow brown
The mower's stubbling scythe clogs to his foot
The ever-eking whisp
With sharp and sudden jerk,
Till into formal rows the russet shocks
Crowd the blank field to thatch time-weathered barns
And hovels rude repair
Stripped by disturbing winds,

While from the rustling scythe the haunted hare
Scampers circuitous with startled ears
Pricked up, then squat, as by
She brushes to the woods
Where seeded grass breast-high and undisturbed
Form pleasant clumps through which the suthering winds
Softens her rigid fears
And lulls to calm repose.

Wild sorceress, me thy restless mood delights
More than the stir of summer's crowded scenes
Where jostled in the din

Joy palled my ear with song,
Heart-sickening for the silence that is thine,
Not broken inharmoniously as now
That lone and vagrant bee
Booms faint with weary chime

And filtering winds thin winnow through the woods
In tremulous noise that bids at every breath
Some sickly cankered leaf
Let go its hold and die.
And now the bickering storm with sudden start
In flirting fits of anger carps aloud,
Thee urging to thine end,
Sore wept by troubled skies,

And yet—sublime in grief—thy thoughts delight
To show me visions of most gorgeous dyes,
Haply forgetting now
They but prepare thy shroud;
Thy pencil dashing its excess of shades,
Improvident of waste till every bough
Burns with thy mellow touch
Disorderly divine.

Soon must I view thee as a pleasant dream
Droop faintly and so sicken for thine end,
As sad the winds sink low
In dirges for their queen,
While in the moment of their weary pause,
To cheer thy bankrupt pomp the willing lark
Starts from his shielding clod,
Snatching sweet scraps of song.

Thy life is waning now and silence tries
To mourn but meets no sympathy in sounds,
As stooping low she bends,
Forming with leaves thy grave;
To sleep inglorious there mid tangled woods
Till parch-lipped summer pines in drought away,
Then from thine ivied trance
Awake to glories new.

The Nightingale's Nest

Up this green woodland-ride let's softly rove
And list the nightingale—she dwells just here.
Hush! let the wood-gate softly clap for fear
The noise might drive her from her home of love,
For here I've heard her many a merry year—
At morn, at eve, nay, all the livelong day,
As though she lived on song. This very spot,
Just where that old-man's-beard all wildly trails
Rude arbours o'er the road and stops the way—
And where that child its bluebell flowers hath got,
Laughing and creeping through the mossy rails—
There have I hunted like a very boy,
Creeping on hands and knees through matted thorn
To find her nest and see her feed her young.
And vainly did I many hours employ:
All seemed as hidden as a thought unborn.
And where those crimping fern-leaves ramp among
The hazel's under-boughs, I've nestled down
And watched her while she sung, and her renown
Hath made me marvel that so famed a bird
Should have no better dress than russet brown.
Her wings would tremble in her ecstasy
And feathers stand on end as 'twere with joy
And mouth wide open to release her heart

Of its out-sobbing songs. The happiest part
Of summer's fame she shared, for so to me
Did happy fancies shapen her employ,
But if I touched a bush or scarcely stirred,
All in a moment stopped. I watched in vain:
The timid bird had left the hazel bush
And at a distance hid to sing again.
Lost in a wilderness of listening leaves,
Rich ecstasy would pour its luscious strain
Till envy spurred the emulating thrush
To start less wild and scarce inferior songs,
For while of half the year care him bereaves
To damp the ardour of his speckled breast,
The nightingale to summer's life belongs
And naked trees and winter's nipping wrongs
Are strangers to her music and her rest.
Her joys are evergreen, her world is wide—
Hark! there she is as usual—let's be hush—
For in this blackthorn-clump, if rightly guessed,
Her curious house is hidden. Part aside
These hazel branches in a gentle way
And stoop right cautious 'neath the rustling boughs,
For we will have another search today
And hunt this fern-strewn thorn clump round and round,
And where this seeded wood-grass idly bows
We'll wade right through, it is a likely nook:
In such like spots and often on the ground,
They'll build, where rude boys never think to look.
Ay, as I live—her secret nest is here,
Upon this whitethorn stulp. I've searched about
For hours in vain—there, put that bramble by—
Nay, trample on its branches and get near.

How subtle is the bird! she started out
And raised a plaintive note of danger nigh
Ere we were past the brambles, and now, near
Her nest, she sudden stops—as choking fear
That might betray her home. So even now
We'll leave it as we found it: safety's guard
Of pathless solitudes shall keep it still.
See there—she's sitting on the old oak bough,
Mute in her fears; our presence doth retard
Her joys, and doubt turns every rapture chill.
Sing on, sweet bird, may no worse hap befall
Thy visions than the fear that now deceives.
We will not plunder music of its dower
Nor turn this spot of happiness to thrall,
For melody seems hid in every flower
That blossoms near thy home—these harebells all
Seem bowing with the beautiful in song
And gaping cuckoo-flower with spotted leaves
Seems blushing with the singing it has heard.
How curious is the nest: no other bird
Uses such loose materials or weaves
Its dwelling in such spots—dead oaken leaves
Are placed without and velvet moss within
And little scraps of grass and, scant and spare,
What scarcely seem materials, down and hair.
For from man's haunts she nothing seems to win,
Yet nature is the builder and contrives
Homes for her children's comfort even here
Where solitude's disciples spend their lives
Unseen, save when a wanderer passes near
That loves such pleasant places. Deep adown
The nest is made, a hermit's mossy cell.

Snug lie her curious eggs in number five
Of deadened green or rather olive-brown,
And the old prickly thorn-bush guards them well.
So here we'll leave them, still unknown to wrong,
As the old woodland's legacy of song.

The Eternity of Nature

Leaves from eternity are simple things
To the world's gaze—whereto a spirit clings
Sublime and lasting. Trampled underfoot,
The daisy lives and strikes its little root
Into the lap of time: centuries may come
And pass away into the silent tomb
And still the child hid in the womb of time
Shall smile and pluck them when this simple rhyme
Shall be forgotten like a churchyard stone
Or lingering lie unnoticed and alone.
When eighteen hundred years, our common date,
Grow many thousands in their marching state,
Ay, still the child with pleasure in his eye
Shall cry—the daisy! a familiar cry—
And run to pluck it, in the self-same state
As when time found it in his infant date
And like a child himself when all was new
Might smile with wonder and take notice too.
Its little golden bosom frilled with snow
Might win e'en Eve to stoop adown and show
Her partner Adam in the silky grass
This little gem that smiled where pleasure was
And, loving Eve, from Eden followed ill
And bloomed with sorrow and lives smiling still.

As once in Eden under heaven's breath,
So now on earth and on the lap of death
It smiles for ever. Cowslips' golden blooms
That in the closen and the meadow comes
Shall come when kings and empires fade and die,
And in the meadows as time's partners lie
As fresh two thousand years to come as now,
With those five crimson spots upon its brow.
And little brooks that hum a simple lay
In green unnoticed spots, from praise away,
Shall sing when poets in time's darkness hid
Shall lie like memory in a pyramid,
Forgetting yet not all forgot, though lost
Like a thread's end in ravelled windings crossed.
And the small bumble-bee shall hum as long
As nightingales, for time protects the song;
And nature is their soul, to whom all clings
Of fair or beautiful in lasting things.
The little robin in the quiet glen,
Hidden from fame and all the strife of men,
Sings unto time a pastoral and gives
A music that lives on and ever lives.
Both spring and autumn years rich bloom and fade,
Longer than songs that poets ever made.
And think ye these time's playthings? Pass, proud skill,
Time loves them like a child and ever will,
And so I worship them in bushy spots
And sing with them when all else notice not,
And feel the music of their mirth agree
With that sooth quiet that bestirs in me.
And if I touch aright that quiet tone,
That soothing truth that shadows forth their own,

Then many a year shall grow in after-days
And still find hearts to love my quiet lays.
Yet cheering mirth with thoughts sung not for fame
But for the joy that with their utterance came,
That inward breath of rapture urged not loud—
Birds, singing lone, fly silent past a crowd—
So in these pastoral spots which childish time
Makes dear to me, I wander out and rhyme.
What time the dewy morning's infancy
Hangs on each blade of grass and every tree,
And sprents the red thighs of the bumble-bee
Who 'gins betimes unwearied minstrelsy,
Who breakfasts, dines and most divinely sups
With every flower save golden buttercups—
On their proud bosoms he will never go
And passes by with scarcely 'How do ye do?'
So in their showy shining gaudy cells
Maybe the summer's honey never dwells.
Her ways are mysteries: all yet endless youth
Lives in them all, unchangeable as truth.
With the odd number five, strange nature's laws
Plays many freaks nor once mistakes the cause;
And in the cowslip-peeps this very day
Five spots appear, which time ne'er wears away
Nor once mistakes the counting—look within
Each peep, and five, nor more nor less, is seen.
And trailing bindweed with its pinky cup
Five leaves of paler hue goes streaking up;
And birds a many keep the rule alive
And lay five eggs, nor more nor less than five.
And flowers, how many own that mystic power
With five leaves ever making up the flower!

The five-leaved grass, trailing its golden cup
Of flowers—five leaves make all for which I stoop.
And bryony in the hedge that now adorns
The tree to which it clings, and now the thorns,
Owns five-starred pointed leaves of dingy white;
Count which I will, all make the number right.
And spreading goose-grass, trailing all abroad
In leaves of silver green about the road—
Five leaves make every blossom all along.
I stoop for many, none are counted wrong.
'Tis nature's wonder and her maker's will,
Who bade earth be and order owns him still,
As that superior power who keeps the key
Of wisdom, power and might through all eternity.

Emmonsales Heath

In thy wild garb of other times
I find thee lingering still;
Furze o'er each lazy summit climbs
At nature's easy will.

Grasses that never knew a scythe
Wave all the summer long;
And wild weed blossoms waken blithe,
That ploughmen never wrong.

Stern industry with stubborn toil
And wants unsatisfied
Still leaves untouched thy maiden soil
In its unsullied pride.

The birds still find their summer shades
To build their nests again,
And the poor hare its rushy glade
To hide from savage men.

Nature its family protects
In thy security,
And blooms that love what man neglects
Find peaceful homes in thee.

The wild rose scents the summer air
And woodbines weave in bowers
To glad the swain sojourning there
And maidens gathering flowers.

Creation's steps one's wandering meets
Untouched by those of man:
Things seem the same in such retreats
As when the world began.

Furze, ling and brake all mingling free
And grass for ever green—
All seem the same old things to be
As they have ever been.

The dyke o'er such neglected ground,
One's weariness to soothe,
Still wildly winds its lawless bound
And chafes the pebble smooth,

Crooked and rude as when at first
Its waters learned to stray
And from their mossy fountain burst,
It washed itself a way.

O who can pass such lovely spots
Without a wish to stray
And leave life's cares awhile forgot
To muse an hour away?

I've often met with places rude,
Nor failed their sweets to share,

But passed an hour with solitude
And left my blessing there.

He that can meet the morning wind
And o'er such places roam,
Nor leave a lingering wish behind
To make their peace his home—

His heart is dead to quiet hours
Nor love his mind employs,
Poesy with him ne'er shares its flowers
Nor solitude its joys.

O there are spots amid thy bowers
Which nature loves to find,
Where spring drops round her earliest flowers
Unchecked by winter's wind,

Where cowslips wake the child's surprise,
Sweet peeping ere their time,
Ere April spreads her dappled skies
'Mid morning's powdered rime.

I've stretched my boyish walks to thee
When May-day's paths were dry,
When leaves had nearly hid each tree
And grass greened ankle-high,

And mused the sunny hours away
And thought of little things
That children mutter o'er their play
When fancy tries its wings.

Joy nursed me in her happy moods
And all life's little crowd
That haunt the waters, fields and woods
Would sing their joys aloud.

I thought how kind that mighty power
Must in his splendour be,
Who spread around my boyish hour
Such gleams of harmony,

Who did with joyous rapture fill
The low as well as high
And made the pismires round the hill
Seem full as blest as I.

Hope's sun is seen of every eye;
The halo that it gives
In nature's wide and common sky
Cheers everything that lives.

Decay: A Ballad

O poesy is on the wane,
For fancy's visions all unfitting;
I hardly know her face again,
Nature herself seems on the flitting.
The fields grow old and common things—
The grass, the sky, the winds a-blowing
And spots where still a beauty clings—
Are sighing 'Going! all a-going!'
O poesy is on the wane,
I hardly know her face again.

The bank with brambles overspread
And little molehills round about it
Was more to me than laurel shades
With paths and gravel finely clouted,
And streaking here and streaking there
Through shaven grass and many a border
With rutty lanes had no compare
And heaths were in a richer order.
But poesy is on the wane,
I hardly know her face again.

I sat with love by pasture streams—
Ay, beauty's self was sitting by—
Till fields did more than Edens seem,

Nor could I tell the reason why.
I often drank when not a-dry
To pledge her health in draughts divine;
Smiles made it nectar from the sky,
Love turned e'en water into wine.
O poesy is on the wane,
I cannot find her face again.

The sun those mornings used to find
When clouds were other-country mountains
And heaven looked upon the mind
With groves and rocks and mottled fountains.
These heavens are gone, the mountains grey
Turned mist, the sun a homeless ranger
Pursuing on a naked way
Unnoticed like a very stranger.
O poesy is on the wane,
Nor love nor joy is mine again.

Love's sun went down without a frown;
For very joy it used to grieve us.
I often think that west is gone;
Ah, cruel time, to undeceive us!
The stream it is a naked stream,
Where we on Sundays used to ramble;
The sky hangs o'er a broken dream,
The brambles dwindled to a bramble.
O poesy is on the wane,
I cannot find her haunts again.

Mere withered stalks and fading trees
And pastures spread with hills and rushes
Are all my fading vision sees.

Gone, gone is rapture's flooding gushes
When mushrooms they were fairy bowers,
Their marble pillars overswelling,
And danger paused to pluck the flowers
That in their swarthy rings were dwelling.
But poesy's spells are on the wane,
Nor joy nor fear is mine again.

Ay, poesy hath passed away
And fancy's visions undeceive us;
The night hath ta'en the place of day
And why should passing shadows grieve us?
I thought the flowers upon the hills
Were flowers from Adam's open gardens,
And I have had my summer thrills
And I have had my heart's rewardings—
So poesy is on its wane,
I hardly know her face again.

And friendship it hath burned away
Like to a very ember cooling,
A make-believe on April day
That sent the simple heart a-fooling,
Mere jesting in an earnest way,
Deceiving on and still deceiving,
And hope is but a fancy-play
And joy the art of true believing—
For poesy is on the wane,
O could I feel her faith again.

The Pettichap's Nest

Well, in my many walks I rarely found
A place less likely for a bird to form
Its nest—close by the rut-gulled wagon road
And on the almost bare foot-trodden ground
With scarce a clump of grass to keep it warm,
And not a thistle spreads its spears abroad
Or prickly bush to shield it from harm's way,
And yet so snugly made that none may spy
It out save accident—and you and I
Had surely passed it in our walk to day
Had chance not led us by it—nay e'en now,
Had not the old bird heard us trampling by
And fluttered out, we had not seen it lie
Brown as the roadway side—small bits of hay
Plucked from the old propped-haystack's pleachy brow
And withered leaves make up its outward walls
That from the snub-oak dotterel yearly falls
And in the old hedge-bottom rot away.
Built like a oven with a little hole
Hard to discover that snug entrance wins,
Scarcely admitting e'en two fingers in,
And lined with feathers warm as silken stole
And soft as seats of down for painless ease
And full of eggs scarce bigger e'en than peas.

Here's one most delicate with spots as small
As dust—and of a faint and pinky red.
—Well, let them be and safety guard them well
For fear's rude paths around are thickly spread
And they are left to many dangers' ways
When green grasshoppers' jumps might break the shells,
While lowing oxen pass them morn and night
And restless sheep around them hourly stray
And no grass springs but hungry horses bite,
That trample past them twenty times a day.
Yet, like a miracle, in safety's lap
They still abide unhurt and out of sight.
—Stop, here's the bird—that woodman at the gap
Hath frit it from the hedge—'tis olive green—
Well, I declare, it is the pettichap!
Not bigger than the wren and seldom seen:
I've often found their nests in chance's way
When I in pathless woods did idly roam,
But never did I dream until today
A spot like this would be her chosen home.

The Yellowhammer's Nest

Just by the wooden brig a bird flew up,
Frit by the cowboy as he scrambled down
To reach the misty dewberry—let us stoop
And seek its nest—the brook we need not dread,
'Tis scarcely deep enough a bee to drown,
So it sings harmless o'er its pebbly bed
—Ay here it is, stuck close beside the bank
Beneath the bunch of grass that spindles rank
Its husk seeds tall and high—'tis rudely planned
Of bleachèd stubbles and the withered fare
That last year's harvest left upon the land,
Lined thinly with the horse's sable hair.
Five eggs, pen-scribbled o'er with ink their shells
Resembling writing scrawls which fancy reads
As nature's poesy and pastoral spells—
They are the yellowhammer's and she dwells
Most poet-like where brooks and flowery weeds
As sweet as Castaly to fancy seems
And that old molehill like as Parnass' hill
On which her partner haply sits and dreams
O'er all her joys of song—so leave it still
A happy home of sunshine, flowers and streams.
Yet in the sweetest places cometh ill,
A noisome weed that burthens every soil;

For snakes are known with chill and deadly coil
To watch such nests and seize the helpless young,
And like as though the plague became a guest,
Leaving a houseless home, a ruined nest—
And mournful hath the little warblers sung
When such like woes hath rent its little breast.

The Skylark

The rolls and harrows lie at rest beside
The battered road, and spreading far and wide
Above the russet clods the corn is seen
Sprouting its spiry points of tender green
Where squats the hare, to terrors wide awake,
Like some brown clod the harrows failed to break,
While 'neath the warm hedge boys stray far from home
To crop the early blossoms as they come
Where buttercups will make them eager run,
Opening their golden caskets to the sun
To see who shall be first to pluck the prize;
And from their hurry up the skylark flies
And o'er her half-formed nest with happy wings
Winnows the air—till in the cloud she sings,
Then hangs, a dust spot in the sunny skies,
And drops and drops till in her nest she lies,
Where boys unheeding past—ne'er dreaming then
That birds which flew so high would drop again
To nests upon the ground where anything
May come at to destroy. Had they the wing
Like such a bird, themselves would be too proud
And build on nothing but a passing cloud,
As free from danger as the heavens are free
From pain and toil—there would they build and be

And sail about the world to scenes unheard
Of and unseen—O were they but a bird,
So think they while they listen to its song,
And smile and fancy and so pass along
While its low nest moist with the dews of morn
Lies safely with the leveret in the corn.

First Love's Recollections

First love will with the heart remain
When all its hopes are by,
As frail rose blossoms still retain
Their fragrance till they die.
And joy's first dreams will haunt the mind
With shades from whence they sprung,
As summer leaves the stems behind
On which spring's blossoms hung.

Mary, I dare not call thee dear,
I've lost that right so long,
Yet once again I vex thine ear
With memory's idle song.
Had time and change not blotted out
The love of former days,
Thou wert the last that I should doubt
Of pleasing with my praise.

When honied tokens from each tongue
Told with what truth we loved,
How rapturous to thy lips I clung
Whilst nought but smiles reproved;
But now methinks if one kind word
Were whispered in thine ear,

Thou'dst startle like an untamed bird
And blush with wilder fear.

How loath to part, how fond to meet,
Had we two used to be;
At sunset with what eager feet
I hastened on to thee;
Scarce nine days passed us ere we met
In spring, nay wintry weather;
Now nine years' suns have risen and set
Nor found us once together.

Thy face was so familiar grown,
Thyself so often by,
A moment's memory when alone
Would bring thee to mine eye.
But now my very dreams forget
That witching look to trace;
Though there thy beauty lingers yet,
It wears a stranger's face.

I felt a pride to name thy name,
But now that pride hath flown;
My words e'en seem to blush for shame
That own I love thee on.
I felt I then thy heart did share,
Nor urged a binding vow,
But much I doubt if thou couldst spare
One word of kindness now.

And what is now my name to thee,
Though once nought seemed so dear?

Perhaps a jest in hours of glee
To please some idle ear.
And yet like counterfeits with me
Impressions linger on,
Though all the gilded finery
That passed for truth is gone.

Ere the world smiled upon my lays
A sweeter meed was mine,
Thy blushing look of ready praise
Was raised at every line;
But now methinks thy fervent love
Is changed to scorn severe
And songs that other hearts approve
Seem discord to thine ear.

When last thy gentle cheek I pressed
And heard thee feign adieu,
I little thought that seeming jest
Would prove a word so true.
A fate like this hath oft befell
E'en loftier hopes than ours:
Spring bids full many buds to swell
That ne'er can grow to flowers.

Summer Moods

I love at eventide to walk alone
Down narrow lanes o'erhung with dewy thorn
Where, from the long grass underneath, the snail
Jet black creeps out and sprouts his timid horn.
I love to muse o'er meadows newly mown
Where withering grass perfumes the sultry air,
Where bees search round with sad and weary drone
In vain for flowers that bloomed but newly there,
While in the juicy corn the hidden quail
Cries 'wet my foot' and hid as thoughts unborn
The fairylike and seldom-seen landrail
Utters 'craik craik' like voices underground,
Right glad to meet the evening's dewy veil
And see the light fade into glooms around.

Evening Schoolboys

Harken that happy shout—the schoolhouse door
Is open thrown and out the younkers teem.
Some run to leapfrog on the rushy moor
And others dabble in the shallow stream,
Catching young fish and turning pebbles o'er
For muscle clams—Look in that sunny gleam
Where the retiring sun that rests the while
Streams through the broken hedge—How happy seem
Those schoolboy friendships leaning o'er the stile,
Both reading in one book—anon a dream
Rich with new joys doth their young hearts beguile
And the books pocketed right hastily.
Ah happy boys, well may ye turn and smile
When joys are yours that never cost a sigh.

The Shepherd Boy

Pleased in his loneliness he often lies
Telling glad stories to his dog—and e'en
His very shadow that the loss supplies
Of living company. Full oft he'll lean
By pebbled brooks and dream with happy eyes
Upon the fairy pictures spread below,
Thinking the shadowed prospects real skies
And happy heavens where his kindred go.
Oft we may track his haunts where he hath been
To spend the leisure which his toils bestow
By 'nine-peg-morris' nicked upon the green
Or flower-stuck gardens never meant to grow
Or figures cut on trees his skill to show
Where he a prisoner from a shower hath been.

Lord Byron

A splendid sun hath set—when shall our eyes
Behold a morn so beautiful arise
As that which gave his mighty genius birth
And all eclipsed the lesser lights on earth?
His first young burst of twilight did declare
Beyond that haze a sun was rising there,
As when the morn to usher in the day
Speeds from the east in sober garb of grey
At first, till warming into wild delight
She casts her mantle off and shines in light.
The labours of small minds an age may dream
And be but shadows on time's running stream,
While genius in an hour makes what shall be
The next a portion of eternity.

To the Memory of Bloomfield

Sweet unassuming minstrel, not to thee
The dazzling fashions of the day belong:
Nature's wild pictures, field and cloud and tree
And quiet brooks far distant from the throng
In murmurs tender as the toiling bee
Make the sweet music of thy gentle song.
Well, nature owns thee: let the crowd pass by,
The tide of fashion is a stream too strong
For pastoral brooks that gently flow and sing,
But nature is their source, and earth and sky
Their annual offering to her current bring.
Thy gentle muse and memory need no sigh,
For thine shall murmur on to many a spring
When their proud streams are summer-burnt and dry.

Beans in Blossom

The south-west wind, how pleasant in the face
It breathes, while sauntering in a musing pace
I roam these new-ploughed fields, and by the side
Of this old wood where happy birds abide
And the rich blackbird through his golden bill
Utters wild music when the rest are still:
Now luscious comes the scent of blossomed beans
That o'er the path in rich disorder leans,
Mid which the bees in busy songs and toils
Load home luxuriantly their yellow spoils;
The herd cows toss the molehills in their play;
And often stand the stranger's steps at bay
Mid clover blossoms red and tawny-white,
Strong-scented with the summer's warm delight.

To De Wint

De Wint! I would not flatter nor would I
Pretend to critic-skill in this thine art,
Yet in thy landscapes I can well descry
Thy breathing hues as nature's counterpart.
No painted freaks, no wild romantic sky,
No rocks nor mountains as the rich sublime,
Hath made thee famous, but the sunny truth
Of nature that doth mark thee for all time,
Found on our level pastures—spots, forsooth,
Where common skill sees nothing deemed divine.
Yet here a worshipper was found in thee,
Where thy young pencil worked such rich surprise
That rushy flats befringed with willow tree
Rivalled the beauties of Italian skies.

Sudden Shower

Black grows the southern sky betokening rain
And humming hive-bees homeward hurry by;
They feel the change—so let us shun the grain
And take the broad road while our feet are dry.
Ay, there some dropples moistened in my face
And pattered on my hat—'tis coming nigh—
Let's look about and find a sheltering place.
The little things around, like you and I,
Are hurrying through the grass to shun the shower.
Here stoops an ash tree—hark, the wind gets high,
But never mind, this ivy for an hour,
Rain as it may, will keep us dryly here.
That little wren knows well his sheltering bower
Nor leaves his dry house though we come so near.

Stepping Stones

The stepping stones that stride the meadow-streams
Look picturesque amid spring's golden gleams
Where steps the traveller with a weary pace,
And boy with laughing leisure in his face
Sits on the midmost stone in very whim
To catch the struttles that beneath him swim,
While those across the hollow lakes are bare
And winter floods no more rave dangers there,
But mid the scum left where it roared and fell
The schoolboy hunts to find the pooty shell.
Yet there the boisterous geese with golden broods
Hiss fierce and daring in their summer moods:
The boys pull off their hats while passing by,
In vain to fright—themselves being forced to fly.

Pleasant Places

Old stone pits with veined ivy overhung,
Wild crooked brooks o'er which is rudely flung
A rail and plank that bends beneath the tread,
Old narrow lanes where trees meet overhead,
Path-stiles on which a steeple we espy
Peeping and stretching in the distant sky,
And heaths o'erspread with furze-bloom's sunny shine
Where wonder pauses to exclaim 'divine!'
Old ponds dim-shadowed with a broken tree—
These are the picturesque of taste to me,
While painting winds, to make complete the scene
In rich confusion mingles every green,
Waving the sketchy pencil in their hands,
Shading the living scenes to fairy lands.

On Leaving the Cottage of my Birth

I've left mine own old home of homes,
Green fields and every pleasant place;
The summer like a stranger comes,
I pause and hardly know her face;
I miss the hazel's happy green,
The bluebell's quiet-hanging blooms,
Where envy's sneer was never seen,
Where staring malice never comes.

I miss the heath, its yellow furze,
Molehills and rabbit tracks that lead
Through besom-ling and teasel burrs
That spread a wilderness indeed,
The woodland oaks and all below
That their white-powdered branches shield,
The mossy paths—the very crow
Croaked music in my native field.

I sit me in my corner chair
That seems to feel itself from home,
And hear bird-music here and there
From 'awthorn hedge and orchard come,
I hear but all is strange and new
—I sat on my old bench last June,

The sailing puddock's shrill 'peelew'
O'er Royce Wood seemed a sweeter tune.

I walk adown the narrow lane,
The nightingale is singing now,
But like to me she seems at loss
For Royce Wood and its shielding bough.
I lean upon the window sill,
The trees and summer happy seem,
Green, sunny green they shine—but still
My heart goes far away to dream

Of happiness, and thoughts arise
With home-bred pictures many a one:
Green lanes that shut out burning skies
And old crook'd stiles to rest upon;
Above them hangs the maple tree,
Below grass swells a velvet hill
And little footpaths sweet to see
Goes seeking sweeter places still,

With by and by a brook to cross,
O'er which a little arch is thrown.
No brook is here: I feel the loss
From home and friends and all alone.
The stone pit with its shelving sides
Seemed hanging rocks in my esteem,
I miss the prospect far and wide
From Langley Bush, and so I seem

Alone and in a stranger scene
Far far from spots my heart esteems:

The closen with their ancient green,
Heaths, woods and pastures, sunny streams.
The hawthorns here are hung with may
But still they seem in deader green;
The sun e'en seems to lose its way
Nor knows the quarter it is in.

I dwell on trifles like a child,
I feel as ill becomes a man,
And still my thoughts like weedlings wild
Grow up to blossom where they can:
They turn to places known so long
And feel that joy was dwelling there,
So homebred pleasure fills the song
That has no present joys to heir.

Northborough, June 20, 1832

Poems written
at Northborough

To the Snipe

Lover of swamps,
The quagmire overgrown
With hassock-tufts of sedge—where fear encamps
Around thy home alone

The trembling grass
Quakes from the human foot
Nor bears the weight of man to let him pass
Where thou alone and mute

Sittest at rest
In safety 'neath the clump
Of huge flag-forest that thy haunts invest
Or some old sallow stump

Thriving on seams
That tiny islands swell,
Just hilling from the mud and rancid streams,
Suiting thy nature well—

For here thy bill,
Suited by wisdom good
Of rude unseemly length, doth delve and drill
The gelid mass for food,

And here, mayhap,
When summer suns hath dressed
The moor's rude, desolate and spongy lap,
May hide thy mystic nest—

Mystic indeed,
For isles that ocean make
Are scarcely more secure for birds to build
Than this flag-hidden lake.

Boys thread the woods
To their remotest shades,
But in these marshy flats, these stagnant floods,
Security pervades

From year to year,
Places untrodden lie
Where man nor boy nor stock hath ventured near
—Nought gazed on but the sky

And fowl that dread
The very breath of man,
Hiding in spots that never knew his tread—
A wild and timid clan,

Widgeon and teal
And wild duck, restless lot
That from man's dreaded sight will ever steal
To the most dreary spot.

Here tempests howl
Around each flaggy plot

Where they who dread man's sight, the waterfowl,
Hide and are frighted not.

'Tis power divine
That heartens them to brave
The roughest tempest and at ease recline
On marshes or the wave;

Yet instinct knows
Not safety's bounds—to shun
The firmer ground where stalking fowler goes
With searching dogs and gun

By tepid springs
Scarcely one stride across:
Though brambles from its edge a shelter flings,
Thy safety is at loss.

And never choose
The little sinky foss
Streaking the moors whence spa-red water spews
From puddles fringed with moss:

Freebooters there,
Intent to kill or slay,
Startle with cracking guns the trepid air
And dogs thy haunts betray.

From danger's reach
Here thou art safe to roam
Far as these washy flag-sown marshes stretch,
A still and quiet home.

In these thy haunts
I've gleaned habitual love;
From the vague world where pride and folly taunts
I muse and look above.

Thy solitudes
The unbounded heaven esteems
And here my heart warms into higher moods
And dignifying dreams.

I see the sky
Smile on the meanest spot,
Giving to all that creep or walk or fly
A calm and cordial lot.

Thine teaches me
Right feelings to employ:
That in the dreariest places peace will be
A dweller and a joy.

[The Lament of Swordy Well]

Petitioners are full of prayers
To fall in pity's way,
But if her hand the gift forbears
They'll sooner swear than pray.
They're not the worst to want, who lurch
On plenty with complaints,
No more than those who go to church
Are e'er the better saints.

I hold no hat to beg a mite
Nor pick it up when thrown,
No limping leg I hold in sight
But pray to keep my own.
Where profit gets his clutches in,
There's little he will leave;
Gain stooping for a single pin
Will stick it on his sleeve.

For passers-by I never pin
No troubles to my breast,
Nor carry round some names to win
More money from the rest.
I'm Swordy Well, a piece of land
That's fell upon the town,

Who worked me till I couldn't stand
And crush me now I'm down.

In parish bonds I well may wail,
Reduced to every shift;
Pity may grieve at trouble's tale
But cunning shares the gift.
Harvests with plenty on his brow
Leaves losses' taunts with me,
Yet gain comes yearly with the plough
And will not let me be.

Alas dependence, thou'rt a brute
Want only understands;
His feelings wither branch and root
That falls in parish hands.
The muck that clouts the ploughman's shoe,
The moss that hides the stone,
Now I'm become the parish due
Is more than I can own.

Though I'm no man, yet any wrong
Some sort of right may seek,
And I am glad if e'en a song
Gives me the room to speak.
I've got among such grubbling gear
And such a hungry pack,
If I brought harvests twice a year
They'd bring me nothing back.

When war their tyrant prices got,
I trembled with alarms;
They fell and saved my little spot,
Or towns had turned to farms.

Let profit keep an humble place
That gentry may be known;
Let pedigrees their honours trace
And toil enjoy its own.

The silver springs grown naked dykes
Scarce own a bunch of rushes;
When grain got high the tasteless tykes
Grubbed up trees, banks and bushes,
And me, they turned me inside out
For sand and grit and stones
And turned my old green hills about
And picked my very bones.

These things that claim my own as theirs
Were born but yesterday,
But ere I fell to town affairs
I were as proud as they:
I kept my horses, cows and sheep
And built the town below
Ere they had cat or dog to keep—
And then to use me so.

Parish allowance, gaunt and dread,
Had it the earth to keep,
Would even pine the bees to dead
To save an extra keep.
Pride's workhouse is a place that yields
From poverty its gains,
And mine's a workhouse for the fields,
A-starving the remains.

The bees fly round in feeble rings
And find no blossom by,

Then thrum their almost-weary wings
Upon the moss and die.
Rabbits that find my hills turned o'er
Forsake my poor abode—
They dread a workhouse like the poor
And nibble on the road.

If with a clover bottle now
Spring dares to lift her head,
The next day brings the hasty plough
And makes me misery's bed.
The butterflies may whirr and come,
I cannot keep 'em now,
Nor can they bear my parish home
That withers on my brow.

No, now not e'en a stone can lie,
I'm just whate'er they like;
My hedges like the winter fly
And leave me but the dyke;
My gates are thrown from off the hooks,
The parish thoroughfare:
Lord, he that's in the parish books
Has little wealth to spare.

I couldn't keep a dust of grit
Nor scarce a grain of sand,
But bags and carts claimed every bit
And now they've got the land.
I used to bring the summer's life
To many a butterfly,
But in oppression's iron strife
Dead tussocks bow and sigh.

I've scarce a nook to call my own
For things that creep or fly—
The beetle hiding 'neath a stone
Does well to hurry by.
Stock eats my struggles every day
As bare as any road;
He's sure to be in something's way
If e'er he stirs abroad.

I am no man to whine and beg,
But fond of freedom still
I hang no lies on pity's peg
To bring a grist to mill;
On pity's back I needn't jump,
My looks speak loud alone—
My only tree they've left a stump
And nought remains my own.

My mossy hills gain's greedy hand
And more than greedy mind
Levels into a russet land,
Nor leaves a bent behind.
In summers gone I bloomed in pride,
Folks came for miles to prize
My flowers that bloomed nowhere beside
And scarce believed their eyes.

Yet worried with a greedy pack
They rend and delve and tear
The very grass from off my back—
I've scarce a rag to wear,
Gain takes my freedom all away
Since its dull suit I wore

And yet scorn vows I never pay
And hurts me more and more.

Whoever pays me rent or takes it,
I've neither words or dates;
One makes the law and others break it
And stop my mouth with rates.

And should the price of grain get high—
Lord help and keep it low—
I shan't possess a single fly
Or get a weed to grow;
I shan't possess a yard of ground
To bid a mouse to thrive,
For gain has put me in a pound,
I scarce can keep alive.

I'm not a man, as some may think,
Petitioning for loss
Of cow that died of age's drink
And spavin-foundered horse
For which some beg a list of pelf
And seem on loss to thrive,
But I petition for myself
And beg to keep alive.

There's folks that make a mort of bother
And o'er lost gainings whine,
But, lord, of me I'm this and t'other,
There's no one cares for mine.
They strip the grass from off my back
And take my things away:
I'm robbed by every outlaw pack

[   ]

I own I'm poor like many more
But then the poor mun live,
And many came for miles before
For what I had to give;
But since I fell upon the town
They pass me with a sigh,
I've scarce the room to say 'Sit down'
And so they wander by.

The town that brought me in disgrace
Have got their tales to say;
I ha'n't a friend in all the place
Save one and he's away.
A grubbling man with much to keep
And nought to keep 'em on
Found me a bargain offered cheap
And so my peace was gone.

But when a poor man is allowed
So to enslave another,
Well may the world's tongue prate aloud
How brother uses brother.
I could not keep a bush to stand
For years but what was gone,
And now I ha'n't a foot of land
To keep a rabbit on.

They used to come and feed at night
When danger's day was gone,
And in the morning out of sight
Hide underneath a stone.

I'm fain to shun the greedy pack
That now so tear and brag;

They strip the coat from off my back
And scarcely leave a rag,
That like the parish hurt and hurt
While gain's new suit I wear,
Then swear I never pay 'em for't
And add to my despair.

Though now I seem so full of clack,
Yet when you're riding by
The very birds upon my back
Are not more fain to fly.
I feel so lorn in this disgrace,
God send the grain to fall;
I am the oldest in the place
And the worst-served of all.

Lord bless ye, I was kind to all
And poverty in me
Could always find a humble stall,
A rest and lodging free;
Poor bodies with an hungry ass
I welcomed many a day,
And gave him tether-room and grass
And never said him nay.

There was a time my bit of ground
Made freemen of the slave;
The ass no pindar'd dare to pound
When I his supper gave;
The gypsies' camp was not afraid,
I made his dwelling free,
Till vile enclosure came and made
A parish slave of me.

The gypsies further on sojourn,
No parish bonds they like;
No sticks I own, and would earth burn
I shouldn't own a dyke.
I am no friend to lawless work,
Nor would a rebel be,
And why I call a Christian Turk
Is they are Turks to me.

I am the last
Of all the field that fell;
My name is nearly all that's left
Of what was Swordy Well.

And if I could but find a friend
With no deceit to sham,
Who'd send me some few sheep to tend
And leave me as I am,
To keep my hills from cart and plough
And strife of mongrel men
And as spring found me find me now,
I should look up again.

And save his Lordship's woods that past
The day of danger dwell,
Of all the fields I am the last
That my own face can tell.
Yet, what with stone pits' delving holes
And strife to buy and sell,
My name will quickly be the whole
That's left of Swordy Well.

Snowstorm

What a night: the wind howls, hisses and but stops
To howl more loud while the snow volley keeps
Incessant batter at the window pane,
Making our comfort feel as sweet again;
And in the morning, when the tempest drops,
At every cottage door mountainous heaps
Of snow lies drifted, that all entrance stops
Until the besom and the shovel gains
The path—and leaves a wall on either side.
The shepherd, rambling valleys white and wide,
With new sensations his old memories fills
When hedges left at night no more descried
Are turned to one white sweep of curving hills
And trees turned bushes half their bodies hide.

Bumbarrel's Nest

The oddling bush, close sheltered hedge new-plashed,
Of which spring's early liking makes a guest
First with a shade of green though winter-dashed—
There, full as soon, bumbarrels make a nest
Of mosses grey with cobwebs closely tied
And warm and rich as feather-bed within,
With little hole on its contrary side
That pathway peepers may no knowledge win
Of what her little oval nest contains—
Ten eggs and often twelve, with dusts of red
Soft frittered—and full soon the little lanes
Screen the young crowd and hear the twitt'ring song
Of the old birds who call them to be fed
While down the hedge they hang and hide along.

Open Winter

Where slanting banks are always with the sun
The daisy is in blossom even now
And where warm patches by the hedges run
The cottager when coming home from plough
Brings home a cowslip root in flower to set;
Thus ere the Christmas goes the spring is met
Setting up little tents about the fields
In sheltered spots—primroses when they get
Behind the wood's old roots where ivy shields
Their crimpled curdled leaves will shine and hide
—Cart ruts and horse footings scarcely yield
A slur for boys just crizzled and that's all.
Frost shoots his needles by the small dyke side
And snow in scarce a feather's seen to fall.

[double sonnet on the Marten]

The marten cat, long-shagged, of courage good,
Of weasel shape, a dweller in the wood,
With badger hair long-shagged and darting eyes
And lower than the common cat in size,
Small head, and running on the stoop,
Snuffing the ground, and hind-parts shouldered up—
He keeps one track and hides in lonely shade
Where print of human foot is scarcely made,
Save when the woods are cut. The beaten track
The woodman's dog will snuff, cock-tailed and black,
Red-legged and spotted over either eye:
Snuffs, barks, and scrats the tree and passes by.
The great brown hornèd owl looks down below
And sees the shaggy marten come and go.

The marten hurries through the woodland gaps
And poachers shoot and make his skin for caps.
When any woodman come and pass the place,
He looks at dogs and scarcely mends his pace.
And gypsies often and bird-nesting boys
Look in the hole and hear a hissing noise;
They climb the tree—such noise they never heard,
And think the great owl is a foreign bird—
When the grey owl, her young ones clothed in down,

Seizes the boldest boy and drives him down.
They try again and pelt to start the fray:
The grey owl comes and drives them all away,
And leaves the marten twisting round his den,
Left free from boys and dogs and noise and men.

[sonnet sequence on Fox and Badger]

The shepherd on his journey heard when nigh
His dog among the bushes barking high;
The ploughman ran and gave a hearty shout,
He found a weary fox and beat him out.
The ploughman laughed and would have ploughed him in,
But the old shepherd took him for the skin.
He lay upon the furrow stretched and dead,
The old dog lay and licked the wounds that bled,
The ploughman beat him till his ribs would crack,
And then the shepherd slung him at his back;
And when he rested, to his dog's surprise,
The old fox started from his dead disguise
And while the dog lay panting in the sedge
He up and snapped and bolted through the hedge.

He scampered to the bushes far away:
The shepherd called the ploughman to the fray,
The ploughman wished he had a gun to shoot,
The old dog barked and followed the pursuit,
The shepherd threw his hook and tottered past,
The ploughman ran but none could go so fast,
The woodman threw his faggot from the way
And ceased to chop and wondered at the fray,
But when he saw the dog and heard the cry

He threw his hatchet, but the fox was by—
The shepherd broke his hook and lost the skin—
He found a badger hole and bolted in.
They tried to dig but safe from danger's way
He lived to chase the hounds another day.

The badger grunting on his woodland track
With shaggy hide and sharp nose scrowed with black
Roots in the bushes and the woods and makes
A great huge burrow in the ferns and brakes;
With nose on ground he runs an awk'ard pace
And anything will beat him in the race:
The shepherd's dog will run him to his den
Followed and hooted by the dogs and men;
The woodman when the hunting comes about
Go round at night to stop the foxes out
And hurrying through the bushes, ferns and brakes
Nor sees the many holes the badger makes
And often through the bushes to the chin
Breaks the old holes and tumbles headlong in.

When midnight comes a host of dogs and men
Go out and track the badger to his den
And put a sack within the hole and lie
Till the old grunting badger passes by:
He comes and hears—they let the strongest loose.
The old fox hears the noise and drops the goose;
The poacher shoots and hurries from the cry
And the old hare half-wounded buzzes by.
They get a forkèd stick to bear him down
And clapped the dogs and bore him to the town
And bait him all the day with many dogs

And laugh and shout and fright the scampering hogs—
He runs along and bites at all he meets;
They shout and holler down the noisy streets.

He turns about to face the loud uproar
And drives the rebels to their very doors—
The frequent stone is hurled where'er they go.
When badgers fight and everyone's a foe,
The dogs are clapped and urged to join the fray,
The badger turns and drives them all away;
Though scarcely half as big, dimute and small,
He fights with dogs for hours and beats them all:
The heavy mastiff, savage in the fray,
Lies down and licks his feet and turns away;
The bulldog knows his match and waxes cold,
The badger grins and never leaves his hold.
He drives the crowd and follows at their heels
And bites them through—the drunkard swears and reels.

The frighted women takes the boys away,
The blackguard laughs and hurries in the fray.
He tries to reach the woods, a awk'ard race,
But sticks and cudgels quickly stop the chase.
He turns again and drives the noisy crowd
And beats the many dogs in noises loud;
He drives away and beats them every one
And then they loose them all and set them on.
He falls as dead and kicked by boys and men,
Then starts and grins and drives the crowd again,
Till kicked and torn and beaten out he lies
And leaves his hold and cackles, groans and dies.

[Field-Mouse's Nest]

I found a ball of grass among the hay
And progged it as I passed and went away
And when I looked I fancied something stirred
And turned again and hoped to catch the bird,
When out an old mouse bolted in the wheat
With all her young ones hanging at her teats.
She looked so odd and so grotesque to me,
I ran and wondered what the thing could be
And pushed the knapweed bunches where I stood.
When the mouse hurried from the crawling brood
The young ones squeaked, and when I went away
She found her nest again among the hay.
The water o'er the pebbles scarce could run
And broad old sexpools glittered in the sun.

[Birds at Evening]

I love to hear the evening crows go by
And see the starnels darken down the sky;
The bleaching stack the bustling sparrow leaves
And plops with merry note beneath the eaves;
The odd and lated pigeon bounces by
As if a wary watching hawk was nigh,
While far, and fearing nothing, high and slow,
The stranger birds to distant places go;
While short of flight the evening robin comes
To watch the maiden sweeping out the crumbs,
Nor fears the idle shout of passing boy
But pecks about the door and sings for joy,
Then in the hovel where the cows are fed
Finds till the morning comes a pleasant bed.

[Trespass]

I dreaded walking where there was no path
And pressed with cautious tread the meadow swath
And always turned to look with wary eye
And always feared the owner coming by;
Yet everything about where I had gone
Appeared so beautiful I ventured on
And when I gained the road where all are free
I fancied every stranger frowned at me
And every kinder look appeared to say
'You've been on trespass in your walk today.'
I've often thought, the day appeared so fine,
How beautiful if such a place were mine;
But, having naught, I never feel alone
And cannot use another's as my own.

Glinton Spire

I love to see the slender spire,
For there the maid of beauty dwells,
And stand again' the hollow tree
And hear the sound of Glinton Bells.

I love to see the boys at play;
The music o'er the summer swells;
I stand among the new-mown hay
And hear the sound of Glinton Bells.

I love the slender spire to see,
For there the maid of beauty dwells,
I think she hears the sound with me
And love to listen Glinton Bells.

And when with songs I used to talk,
I often thought where Mary dwells,
And often took a sabbath walk
And lay and listened Glinton Bells.

I think where Mary's memory stays,
I think where pleasant memory dwells,
I think of happy schoolboy days,
And lie and listen Glinton Bells.

Poems written
at the High Beach Asylum

A Walk in the Forest

I love the forest and its airy bounds
Where friendly Campbell takes his daily rounds,
I love the breakneck hills that headlong go
And leave me high and half the world below,
I love to see the Beach Hill mounting high,
The brook without a bridge and nearly dry.
There's Bucket's Hill, a place of furze and clouds,
Which evening in a golden blaze enshrouds:
I hear the cows go home with tinkling bell
And see the woodman in the forest dwell,
Whose dog runs eager where the rabbit's gone—
He eats the grass, then kicks and hurries on,
Then scrapes for hoarded bone and tries to play
And barks at larger dogs and runs away.

London *versus* Epping Forest

The brakes like young stag's horns come up in spring
And hide the rabbit holes and fox's den;
They crowd about the forest everywhere,
The ling and holly-bush and woods of beech
With room enough to walk and search for flowers.
Then look away and see the Kentish heights:
Nature is lofty in her better mood,
She leaves the world and greatness all behind.
Thus London like a shrub among the hills
Lies hid and lower than the bushes here.
I could not bear to see the tearing plough
Root up and steal the forest from the poor,
But leave to freedom all she loves untamed,
The forest walk enjoyed and loved by all.

The Gypsy Camp

The snow falls deep, the forest lies alone,
The boy goes hasty for his load of brakes,
Then thinks upon the fire and hurries back;
The gypsy knocks his hands and tucks them up
And seeks his squalid camp half hid in snow
Beneath the oak which breaks away the wind
And bushes close with snow like hovel warm.
There stinking mutton roasts upon the coals
And the half-roasted dog squats close and rubs,
Then feels the heat too strong and goes aloof;
He watches well but none a bit can spare,
And vainly waits the morsel thrown away.
'Tis thus they live—a picture to the place,
A quiet, pilfering, unprotected race.

Two songs and some stanzas from
Child Harold

Song

The sun has gone down with a veil on his brow
While I in the forest sit musing alone;
The maiden has been o'er the hills for her cow
While my heart's affections are freezing to stone;
Sweet Mary, I wish that the day was my own
To live in a cottage with beauty and thee;
The past I will not as a mourner bemoan
For absence leaves Mary still dearer to me.

How sweet are the glooms of the midsummer even,
Dark night in the bushes seems going to rest
And the bosom of Mary with fancies is heaving
Where my sorrows and feelings for seasons were blest.
Nor will I repine though in love we're divided,
She in the lowlands and I in the glen
Of these forest beeches—by nature we're guided
And I shall find rest on her bosom again.

How soft the dew falls on the leaves of the beeches,
How fresh the wild flower seems to slumber below,
How sweet are the lessons that nature still teaches,
For truth is her tidings wherever I go.

From school days of boyhood her image was cherished;
In manhood sweet Mary was fairer than flowers,
Nor yet has her name or her memory perished
Though absence like winter o'er happiness lowers.

Though cares still will gather like clouds in my sky,
Though hopes may grow hopeless and fetters recoil,
While the sun of existence sheds light in my eye
I'll be free in a prison and cling to the soil,
I'll cling to the spot where my first love was cherished,
Where my heart, nay my soul, unto Mary I gave,
And when my last hope and existence is perished
Her memory will shine like a sun on my grave.

[*stanzas*]

Mary, thou ace of hearts, thou muse of song,
The pole star of my being and decay;
Earth's coward foes my shattered bark may wrong,
Still thou'rt the sunrise of my natal day—
Born to misfortunes, where no sheltering bay
Keeps off the tempest, wrecked where'er I flee,
I struggle with my fate in trouble strong.
Mary, thy name loved long still keeps me free
Till my lost life becomes a part of thee.

Love is the main spring of existence—it
Becomes a soul whereby I live to love;
On all I see that dearest name is writ.
Falsehood is here—but truth has life above,
Where every star that shines exists in love.

Skies vary in their clouds, the seasons vary
From heat to cold, change cannot constant prove,
The south is bright, but smiles can act contrary:
My guide star gilds the north—and shines with Mary.

My life hath been one love—no, blot it out—
My life hath been one chain of contradictions:
Madhouses, prisons, whore shops—never doubt
But that my life hath had some strong convictions
That such was wrong—religion makes restrictions
I would have followed, but life turned a bubble
And clumb the giant stile of maledictions.
They took me from my wife and to save trouble
I wed again and made the error double.

Yet absence claims them both and keeps them too
And locks me in a shop in spite of law
Among a low-lived set and dirty crew;
Here let the muse oblivion's curtain draw
And let man think—for God hath often saw
Things here too dirty for the light of day,
For in a madhouse there exists no law.
Now stagnant grows my too refinèd clay;
I envy birds their wings to fly away.

How servile is the task to please alone,
Though beauty woo and love inspire the song,
Mere painted beauty with her heart of stone
Thinks the world worships while she flaunts along;
The flower of sunshine, butterfly of song,
Give me the truth of heart in woman's life,
The love to cherish one—and do no wrong

To none. O peace of every care and strife
Is true love in an estimable wife.

How beautiful this hill of fern swells on,
So beautiful the chapel peeps between
The hornbeams with its simple bell—alone
I wander here, hid in a palace green.
Mary is absent, but the forest queen
Nature is with me—morning, noon and gloaming,
I write my poems in these paths unseen
And when among these brakes and beeches roaming
I sigh for truth and home and love and woman.

I sigh for one and two—and still I sigh,
For many are the whispers I have heard
From beauty's lips. Love's soul in many an eye
Hath pierced my heart with such intense regard:
I looked for joy and pain was the reward;
I think of them—I love each girl and boy,
Babes of two mothers—on this velvet sward
And nature thinks in her so sweet employ
While dews fall on each blossom weeping joy.

Here is the chapel-yard enclosed with pales
And oak trees nearly top its little bell;
Here is the little bridge with guiding rail
That leads me on to many a pleasant dell;
The fern-owl chitters like a startled knell
To nature, yet 'tis sweet at evening still—
A pleasant road curves round the gentle swell
Where nature seems to have her own sweet will,
Planting her beech and thorn about the sweet fern hill.

I have had many loves—and seek no more—
These solitudes my last delights shall be:
The leaf-hid forest and the lonely shore
Seem to my mind like beings that are free,
Yet would I had some eye to smile on me,
Some heart where I could make a happy home in—
Sweet Susan that was wont my love to be
And Bessy of the glen—for I've been roaming
With both at morn and noon and dusky gloaming.

Cares gather round. I snap their chains in two
And smile in agony and laugh in tears,
Like playing with a deadly serpent who
Stings to the death—there is no room for fears
Where death would bring me happiness: his shears
Kills cares that hiss to poison many a vein;
The thought to be extinct my fate endears;
Pale death, the grand physician, cures all pain;
The dead rest well—who lived for joys in vain.

[*song*] *Written in a Thunderstorm July 15th 1841*

The heavens are wrath, the thunder's rattling peal
Rolls like a vast volcano in the sky,
Yet nothing starts the apathy I feel
Nor chills with fear eternal destiny—

My soul is apathy, a ruin vast;
Time cannot clear the ruined mass away.
My life is hell—the hopeless die is cast
And manhood's prime is premature decay.

Roll on, ye wrath of thunders, peal on peal,
Till worlds are ruins and myself alone;
Melt heart and soul cased in obdurate steel
Till I can feel that nature is my throne.

I live in love, sun of undying light,
And fathom my own heart for ways of good;
In its pure atmosphere day without night
Smiles on the plains, the forest and the flood.

Smile on, ye elements of earth and sky,
Or frown in thunders as ye frown on me:
Bid earth and its delusions pass away,
But leave the mind as its creator free.

Don Juan: A Poem

'Poets are born'—and so are whores—the trade is
Grown universal: in these canting days
Women of fashion must of course be ladies
And whoring is the business that still pays.
Playhouses, ballrooms—there the masquerade is,
To do what was of old, and nowadays
Their maids, nay wives, so innocent and blooming
Cuckold their spouses to seem honest women.

There's much said about love and more of women.
I wish they were as modest as they seem:
Some borrow husbands till their cheeks are blooming,
Not like the red rose blush—but yellow cream.
Lord, what a while those good days are in coming—
Routs, masques and balls—I wish they were a dream
—I wish for poor men luck, an honest praxis,
Cheap food and clothing, no corn laws or taxes.

I wish—but there is little got by wishing—
I wish that bread and great coats ne'er had risen,
I wish that there was some such word as 'pishun'—
For rhyme sake, for my verses must be dizen
With dresses fine—as hooks with baits for fishing.
I wish all honest men were out of prison;

I wish MP's would spin less yarn—nor doubt
But burn false bills and cross bad taxes out.

I wish young married dames were not so frisky,
Nor hide the ring to make believe they're single;
I wish small beer was half as good as whisky
And married dames with buggers would not mingle.
There's some too cunning far and some too frisky,
And here I want a rhyme, so write down 'jingle'—
And there's such putting in—in whores' crim. con.—
Some mouths would eat forever and eat on.

Childcrn are fond of sucking sugar candy
And maids of sausages—larger the better.
Shopmen are fond of good cigars and brandy,
And I of blunt—and if you change the letter
To C or K it would be quite as handy
And throw the next away—but I'm your debtor
For modesty—yet wishing nought between us,
I'd haul close to a she as Vulcan did to Venus.

I really can't tell what this poem will be
About—nor yet what trade I am to follow.
I thought to buy old wigs—but that will kill me
With cold starvation—as they're beaten hollow.
Long speeches in a famine will not fill me
And madhouse traps still take me by the collar,
So old wig bargains now must be forgotten—
The oil that dressed them fine has made them rotten.

I wish old wigs were done with ere they're mouldy,
I wish—but here's the papers large and lusty

With speeches that full fifty times they've told ye
—Noble Lord John to sweet Miss Fanny Fusty
Is wed—a lie, good reader, I ne'er sold ye
—Prince Albert goes to Germany and must he
Leave the queen's snuff-box where all fools are strumming?
From addled eggs no chickens can be coming.

Whigs strum state fiddle-strings until they snap
With cuckoo, cuckold, cuckoo year by year.
The razor plays it on the barber's strap
—The scissors-grinder thinks it rather queer
That labour won't afford him 'one wee drap'
Of ale or gin or half-and-half or beer
—I wish Prince Albert and the noble dastards
Who wed the wives would get the noble bastards.

I wish Prince Albert on his German journey,
I wish the Whigs were out of office and
Pickled in law books of some good attorney,
For ways and speeches few can understand:
They'll bless ye when in power—in prison scorn ye
And make a man rent his own house and land—
I wish Prince Albert's queen was undefiled
—And every man could get his wife with child.

I wish the devil luck with all my heart
As I would any other honest body;
His bad name passes by me like a f—t
Stinking of brimstone—then like whisky toddy
We swallow sin which seems to warm the heart
—There's no imputing any sin to God—he
Fills hell with work—and isn't it a hard case
To leave old Whigs and give to hell the carcass.

Me-b—ne may throw his wig to little Vicky
And so resign his humbug and his power,
And she with the young princess mount the dickey—
On ass-milk diet for her German tour,
Asses like ministers are rather tricky:
I and the country proves it every hour,
W-ll—gt-n and M-lb—ne in their station,
Cobblers to queens—are physic to the nation.

These batch of toadstools on this rotten tree
Shall be the cabinet of any queen,
Though not such cobblers as her servants be—
They're of God's making, that is plainly seen.
Nor red nor green nor orange—they are free
To thrive and flourish as the Whigs have been,
But come tomorrow—like the Whigs forgotten,
You'll find them withered, stinking, dead and rotten.

Death is an awful thing, it is by God;
I've said so often and I think so now.
'Tis rather droll to see an old wig nod,
Then doze and die, the devil don't know how.
Odd things are wearisome and this is odd—
'Tis better work than kicking up a row.
I'm weary of old Whigs and old Whigs' heirs
And long been sick of teasing God with prayers.

I've never seen the cow turn to a bull,
I've never seen the horse become an ass,
I've never seen an old brawn clothed in wool—
But I have seen full many a bonny lass
And wish I had one now beneath the cool
Of these high elms—Muse, tell me where I was—

O, talk of turning, I've seen Whig and Tory
Turn imps of hell—and all for England's glory.

I love good fellowship and wit and punning,
I love 'true love' and, God my taste defend,
I hate most damnably all sorts of cunning—
I love the Moor and Marsh and Ponders End—
I do not like the song of 'cease your funning,'
I love a modest wife and trusty friend
—Bricklayers want lime as I want rhyme for fill-ups,
So here's a health to sweet Eliza Phillips:

Song

Eliza, now the summer tells
Of spots where love and beauty dwells;
Come and spend a day with me
Underneath the forest tree
Where the restless water flushes
Over mosses, mounds and rushes,
And where love and freedom dwells
With orchis flowers and foxglove bells,
Come dear Eliza, set me free
And o'er the forest roam with me.

Here I see the morning sun
Among the beech tree's shadows run,
That into gold the short sward turns,
Where each bright yellow blossom burns
With hues that would his beams outshine,
Yet nought can match those smiles of thine—

I try to find them all the day
But none are nigh when thou'rt away;
Though flowers bloom now on every hill,
Eliza is the fairest still.

The sun wakes up the pleasant morn
And finds me lonely and forlorn,
Then wears away to sunny noon,
The flowers in bloom, the birds in tune,
While dull and dowie all the year,
No smiles to see, no voice to hear,
I in this forest prison lie
With none to heed my silent sigh
And underneath this beechen tree
With none to sigh for, love, but thee.

Now this new poem is entirely new
As wedding gowns or money from the mint;
For all I know, it is entirely true,
For I would scorn to put a lie in print
—I scorn to lie for princes—so would you—
And ere I shoot, I try my pistol flint:
The cattle salesman knows the way in trying
And feels his bullocks ere he thinks of buying.

Lord bless me, now the day is in the gloaming
And every evil thought is out of sight.
How I should like to purchase some sweet woman
Or else creep in with my two wives tonight—
Surely that wedding day is on the coming.
Absence like physic poisons all delight—

Mary and Martha both an evil omen,
Though both my own—they still belong to no man.

But to our text again—and pray where is it?—
Begin as parsons do at the beginning,
Take the first line, friend, and you cannot miss it:
'Poets are born' and so are whores for sinning
—Here's the court circular—O Lord, is this it?—
Court cards like lists of—not the naked meaning—
Here's Albert going to Germany, they tell us,
And the young queen down in the dumps and jealous.

Now have you seen a tramper on racecourses
Seeking an honest penny as his trade is,
Crying a list of all the running horses
And showing handbills of the sporting ladies?
—In bills of fare you'll find a many courses,
Yet all are innocent as any maid is.
Put these two dishes into one and dress it,
And if there is a meaning—you may guess it.

Don Juan was ambassador from Russia
But had no hand in any sort of tax;
His orders hung like blossoms of the fuchsia
And made the ladies' hearts to melt like wax;
He knew Napoleon and the king of Prussia,
And blowed a cloud o'er spirits, wine or max,
But all his profits turned out losses rather,
To save one orphan which he forced to father.

There's Doctor Bottle-imp who deals in urine,
A keeper of state prisons for the queen,
As great a man as is the Doge of Turin,

And save in London is but seldom seen,
Yclep'd old All-n, mad-brained ladies curing,
Some p-x-d like Flora and but seldom clean.
The new road o'er the forest is the right one
To see red hell and further on the white one.

Earth hells or b-gg-r sh-ps or what you please,
Where men close prisoners are and women ravished,
I've often seen such dirty sights as these,
I've often seen good money spent and lavished
To keep bad houses up for doctors' fees,
And I have known a b-gg-r's tally traversed
Till all his good intents began to falter
   When death brought in his bill and left the halter.

O glorious constitution, what a picking
Ye've had from your tax harvest and your tithe—
Old hens which cluck about that fair young chicken,
Cocks without spurs that yet can crow so blithe:
Truth is shut up in prison while ye're licking
The gold from off the gingerbread—be lithe
In winding that patched broken old state clock up,
Playhouses open—but madhouses lock up.

Give toil more pay where rank starvation lurches
And pay your debts and put your books to rights,
Leave whores and playhouses and fill your churches,
Old cloven-foot your dirty victory fights;
Like theft he still on nature's manor poaches
And holds his feasting on another's rights.
To show plain truth you act in bawdy farces;
Men show their tools—and maids expose their arses.

Now this day is the eleventh of July
And being Sunday I will seek no flaw
In man or woman—but prepare to die.
In two days more I may that ticket draw
And so may thousands more as well as I.
Today is here—the next whoever saw;
 And in a madhouse I can find no mirth pay
 —Next Tuesday used to be Lord Byron's birthday.

Lord Byron, poh—the man wot writes the werses
And is just what he is and nothing more,
Who with his pen lies like the mist disperses
And makes all nothing as it was before,
Who wed two wives and oft the truth rehearses
And might have had some twenty thousand more,
Who has been dead, so fools their lies are giving,
And still in Allen's madhouse caged and living.

If I do wickedness, today being Sunday,
Can I by hearing prayers or singing psalms
Clear off all debts twixt God and man on Monday,
And lie like an old hull that dotage calms?
And is there such a word as Abergundy?—
I've read that poem called the 'Isle of Palms'
—But singing sense, pray tell me if I can
Live an old rogue and die an honest man?

I wish I had a quire of foolscap paper
Hot pressed—and crow pens—how I could endite!
A silver candlestick and green wax taper,
Lord bless me, what fine poems I would write!
The very tailors they would read and caper

And mantua-makers would be all delight.
Though laurel wreaths my brows did ne'er environ,
I think myself as great a bard as Byron.

I have two wives and I should like to see them
Both by my side before another hour;
If both are honest I should like to be them,
For both are fair and bonny as a flower,
And one, O Lord—now do bring in the tea, mem—
Were bards' pens' steamers each of ten horsepower,
I could not bring her beauties fair to weather,
So I've towed both in harbour blest together.

Now i'n't this canto worth a single pound
From anybody's pocket who will buy?
As thieves are worth a halter, I'll be bound;
Now honest reader, take the book and try,
And if as I have said it is not found,
I'll write a better canto by and by—
So, reader, now the money till unlock it
And buy the book and help to fill my pocket.

My dear Eliza Phillips
Having been cooped up in this Hell of a Madhouse till I seem to be disowned by my friends and even forgot by my enemies for there is none to accept my challenges which I have from time to time given to the public I am almost mad in waiting for a better place and better company and all to no purpose—It is well known that I am a prize-fighter by profession and a man that never feared any body in my life either in the ring or out of it—I do not much like to write love letters but this which I am now writing to you is a true one—you know that we have met before and the first opportunity that offers we will meet again—I

am now writing a New Canto of Don Juan which I have taken the liberty to dedicate to you in remembrance of Days gone by and when I have finished it I would send you the vol if I knew how in which is a new Canto of Child Harold also—I am my dear Elize
yours sincerely John Clare

Poems and Prose
written at Northborough,
between two asylums

Recollections of Journey from Essex
[*prose account*]

July 23rd 1841.   Returned home out of Essex and found no Mary—her and her family are as nothing to me now, though she herself was once the dearest of all—and how can I forget.

Journal July 18th 1841.   Sunday. Felt very melancholy—went a walk in the forest in the afternoon—fell in with some gypsies, one of whom offered to assist in my escape from the madhouse by hiding me in his camp to which I almost agreed but told him I had no money to start with but if he would do so I would promise him fifty pounds and he agreed to do so before Saturday. On Friday I went again, but he did not seem so willing so I said little about it. On Sunday I went and they were all gone. I found an old wide-awake hat and an old straw bonnet of the plum-pudding sort was left behind and I put the hat in my pocket thinking it might be useful for another opportunity and as good luck would have it, it turned out to be so.

July 19th   Monday—Did nothing.

July 20th   Reconnoitred the route the gypsy pointed out and found it a legible one to make a movement and having only honest courage and myself in my army I led the way and my troops soon followed, but being careless in mapping down the route as the gypsy told me I missed the lane to Enfield Town and was going down Enfield Highway till I passed 'The Labour in Vain' public house where a person I knew coming out of the door told me the way.

I walked down the lane gently and was soon in Enfield Town and bye and bye on the Great York Road where it was all plain sailing and steering ahead meeting no enemy and fearing none. I reached Stevenage where being night I got over a gate, crossed over the corner of a green paddock where seeing a pond or hollow in the corner I [was] forced to stay off a respectable distance to keep from falling into it, for my legs were nearly knocked up and began to stagger. I scaled some old rotten palings into the yard and then had higher palings to clamber over to get into the shed or hovel, which I did with difficulty being rather weak. And to my good luck I found some trusses of clover piled up about six or more feet square, which I gladly mounted and slept on. There was some trays in the hovel on which I could have reposed had I not found a better bed. I slept soundly but had a very uneasy dream: I thought my first wife lay on my left arm and somebody took her away from my side which made me wake up rather unhappy. I thought as I awoke somebody said 'Mary' but nobody was near. I lay down with my head towards the north to show myself the steering point in the morning.

July 21st   When I awoke daylight was looking in on every side and fearing my garrison might be taken by storm and myself be made prisoner I left my lodging by the way I got in and thanked God for his kindness in procuring it (for anything in a famine is better than nothing and any place that giveth the weary rest is a blessing). I gained the North Road again and steered due north. On the left hand side the road under the bank like a cave I saw a man and boy coiled up asleep, which I hailed and they woke up to tell me the name of the next village. Somewhere on the London side the 'Plough' public house a man passed me on horseback in a slop-frock and said 'here's another of the broken-down haymakers' and threw me a penny to get a half-pint of beer, which I picked up and thanked him for and when I got to the Plough I called for a half-pint and drank it and got a rest and escaped a very heavy shower in the bargain by having a shelter till it was over. Afterwards I would have begged a penny of two drovers who were very saucy so I begged no more of anybody, meet who I would. I passed three or four good-built houses on a hill and a public house on the roadside in the hollow below them. I seemed to pass the mile-stones very quick in the morning but towards night they seemed to be stretched further asunder. I got to a village further on and forgot the name. The road on the left hand was quite overshaded by some trees and quite dry so I sat down half an hour and made a good many wishes for breakfast, but wishes was no hearty meal so I got up as hungry as I sat down. I forget here the names of the villages I passed through but recollect at late evening going through Potton in Bedfordshire where I called in a house to light my pipe in which was a civil old woman and a young country wench making lace on a cushion as round as a globe and a young fellow, all civil people—I asked them a few questions as to the way and where the clergyman and overseer lived, but they scarcely heard me or gave me no answer.

I then went through Potton and happened with a kind-talking coun-tryman who told me the parson lived a good way from where I was—or overseer, I don't know which—so I went on hopping with a crippled foot for the gravel had got into my old shoes, one of which had now nearly lost the sole. Had I found the overseer's house at hand or the parson's I should have gave my name and begged for a shilling to carry me home, but I was forced to brush on penniless and be thankful I had a leg to move on.

I then asked him whether he could tell me of a farmyard anywhere on the road where I could find a shed and some dry straw and he said 'Yes and if you will go with me I will show you the place—it's a pub-lic house on the left hand side the road at the sign of the "Ram".' But seeing a stone or flint heap I longed to rest as one of my feet was very painful, so I thanked him for his kindness and bid him go on. But the good-natured fellow lingered awhile as if wishing to conduct me and then suddenly recollecting that he had a hamper on his shoulder and a lock-up bag in his hand cram full to meet the coach which he feared missing—he started hastily and was soon out of sight. I followed, looking in vain for the countryman's straw bed, and not being able to meet it I lay down by a shed side under some elm trees between the wall and the trees, being a thick row planted some five or six feet from the buildings. I lay there and tried to sleep but the wind came in between them so cold that I lay till I quaked like the ague and quitted the lodging for a better at the Ram, which I could hardly hope to find. It now began to grow dark apace and the odd houses on the road began to light up and show the inside tenants' lots very comfortable and my outside lot very uncomfortable and wretched—still I hobbled forward as well as I could and at last came to the Ram. The shutters were not closed and the lighted windows looked very cheering but I had no money and did not like to go in. There was a sort of shed or gig-house at the end but I did not like to lie there as the people were up—so I still travelled on. The road was very lonely and dark, in places being over-shaded with trees. At length I came to a place where the road branched off into two turnpikes, one to the right about and the other straight forward, and on going by my eye glanced on a milestone standing under the hedge so I heedlessly turned back to read it to see where the other road led to and on doing so I found it led to London. I then suddenly forgot which was north or south and though I narrowly examined both ways I could see no tree or bush or stone heap that I could recollect I had passed so I went on mile after mile almost convinced I was going the same way as I came, and these thoughts were so strong upon me that doubt and hopelessness made me turn so feeble that I was scarcely able to walk, yet I could not sit down or give up but shuffled along till I saw a lamp shining as bright as the moon, which on nearing I found was suspended over a tollgate. Before I got through the man came out with a candle and eyed me narrowly, but having no fear I stopped to ask him whether I was going northward and he said 'when you get through the gate you are,' so I thanked him kindly and went through on the other side and gathered my old strength. As my doubts vanished I soon cheered up and hummed the air of 'highland Mary' as I went on. I at length fell in with an odd house all alone near a wood, but I could not see what the sign was though the sign seemed to stand oddly enough in a sort of trough or spout. There was a large porch over the door and being weary I crept in and glad enough I was to find I could lie with my legs straight. The inmates were all gone to roost, for I could hear them turn over in bed. So I lay at full length on the stones in the porch. I slept here till daylight and felt very much refreshed as I got up. I blest my two wives and both their families when I lay down and when I got up, and when I thought of some former difficulties on a like occasion I could not help blessing the Queen.

[July 22nd & 23rd]   Having passed a lodge on the left hand within a mile and a half or less of a town—I think it might be St Ives but I forget the name—I sat down on a flint heap where I might rest half an hour or more and while sitting here I saw a tall gypsy come out of the lodge gate and make down the road towards where I was sitting. When she got up to me, on seeing she was a young woman of an honest-looking countenance—rather handsome—I spoke to her and asked her a few questions, which she answered readily and with evident good humour, so I got up and went on to the next town with her. She cautioned me on the way to put something in my hat to keep the crown up and said in a lower tone 'You'll be noticed,' but not knowing what she hinted I took no notice and made no reply. At length she pointed to a small tower-church, which she called Shefford Church, and advised me to go on a footway which would take me direct to it and I should shorten my journey fifteen miles by doing so. I would gladly have taken the young woman's advice, feeling that it was honest and a nigh guess towards the truth, but fearing I might lose my way and not be able to find the North Road again I thanked her and told her I should keep to the road, when she bade me 'good-day' and went into a house or shop on the left hand side the road.

I have but a slight recollection of my journey between here and Stilton for I was knocked up and noticed little or nothing. One night I lay in a dyke bottom from the wind and went sleep half an hour when I suddenly awoke and found one side wet through from the sock in the dyke bottom, so I got out and went on. I remember going down a very dark road hung over with trees on both sides very thick, which seemed to extend a mile or two. I then entered a town and some of the chamber windows had candle lights shining in them—I felt so weary here that I [was] forced to sit down on the ground to rest myself awhile and while I sat here a coach that seemed to be heavy laden came rattling up and stopped in the hollow below me and I cannot recollect its ever passing by me. I then got up and pushed onward, seeing little to notice for the road very often looked as stupid as myself and I was very often half asleep as I went. On the third day I satisfied my hunger by eating the grass by the roadside, which seemed to taste something like bread. I was hungry and ate heartily till I was satisfied and in fact the meal seemed to do me good. The next and last day I recollected that I had some tobacco, and my box of lucifers being exhausted I could not light my pipe so I took to chewing tobacco all day and ate the quids when I had done and I was never hungry afterwards. I remember passing through Buckden and going a length of road afterwards but I don't recollect the name of any place until I came to Stilton where I was completely foot-foundered and broken down. When I had got about half way through the town a gravel causeway invited me to rest myself, so I lay down and nearly went sleep. A young woman (so I guessed by the voice) came out of a house and said 'poor creature' and another more elderly said 'O he shams.' But when I got up the latter said 'O no he don't,' as I hobbled along very lame. I heard the voices but never looked back to see where they came from. When I got near the inn at the end of the gravel walk I met two young women and I asked one of them whether the road branching to the right by the end of the inn did not lead to Peterborough and she said 'yes' it did so. As soon as ever I was on it I felt myself in home's way and went on rather more cheerful, though I [was] forced to rest oftener than usual. Before I got to Peterborough a man and woman passed me in a cart and on hailing me as they passed I found they were neighbours from Helpstone where I used to live—I told them I was knocked up which they could easily see and that I had neither ate nor drank anything since I left Essex. When I told my story they clubbed together and threw me fivepence out of the cart. I picked it up and called at a small public house near the bridge where I had two half-pints of ale and two pen'orth of bread and cheese. When I had done I started quite refreshed, only my feet was more crippled than ever and I could scarcely make a walk of it over the stones and being half-ashamed to sit down in the street I [was] forced to keep on the move and got through Peterborough better than I expected. When I got on the high road I rested on the stone heaps as I passed till I was able to go on afresh and by and by I passed Walton and soon reached Werrington and was making for the Beehive as fast as I could when a cart passed me with a man and a woman and a boy in it—when nearing me the woman jumped out and caught fast hold of my hands and wished me to get into the cart but I refused and thought her either drunk or mad. But when I was told it was my second wife Patty I got in and was soon at Northborough, but Mary was not there, neither could I get any information about her further than the old story of her being dead six years ago, which might be taken from a bran new old newspaper printed a dozen years ago, but I took no notice of the blarney having seen her myself about a twelvemonth ago alive and well and as young

as ever—so here I am homeless at home and half gratified to feel I can
be happy anywhere.

> 'May none those marks of my sad fate efface
> For they appeal from tyranny to God'   BYRON

Two songs for
Child Harold

Song A

I've wandered many a weary mile
Love in my heart was burning
To seek a home in Mary's smile
But cold is love's returning
The cold ground was a feather bed
Truth never acts contrary
I had no home above my head
My home was love and Mary

I had no home in early youth
When my first love was thwarted
But if her heart still beats with truth
We'll never more be parted
And changing as her love may be
My own shall never vary
Nor night nor day I'm never free
But sigh for absent Mary

Nor night nor day nor sun nor shade
Week month nor rolling year
Repairs the breach wronged love hath made
There madness—misery here

Life's lease was lengthened by her smiles
—Are truth and love contrary
No ray of hope my life beguiles
I've lost love home and Mary

Song B

Here's where Mary loved to be
And here are flowers she planted
Here are books she loved to see
And here—the kiss she granted

Here on the wall with smiling brow
Her picture used to cheer me
Both walls and rooms are naked now
No Mary's nigh to hear me

The church spire still attracts my eye
And leaves me broken-hearted
Though grief hath worn their channels dry
I sigh o'er days departed

The churchyard where she used to play
My feet could wander hourly
My school walks there was every day
Where she made winter flowery

But where is angel Mary now
Love's secrets none disclose 'em
Her rosy cheeks and broken vow
Live in my aching bosom

[prose sketch]

Closes of greensward and meadow eaten down by cattle about harvest time and pieces of naked water such as ponds lakes and pools without fish make me melancholy to look over it and if ever so cheerful I instantly feel low spirited depressed and wretched—on the contrary pieces of greensward where the hay has been cleared off smooth and green as a bowling green with lakes of water well stocked with fish leaping up in the sunshine and leaving rings widening and quavering on the water with the plunge of a Pike in the weeds driving a host of roach into the clear water slanting now and then towards the top their bellies of silver light in the sunshine—these scenes though I am almost wretched quickly animate my feelings and make me happy as if I was rambling in Paradise and perhaps more so than if I was there where there would still be Eves to trouble us.

[Lines written on St Martin's Day,
11 November 1841, *manuscript text*]

Tis martinmass from rig to rig
Ploughed fields & meadow lands are blea
In hedge & field each restless twig
Is dancing on the naked tree
Flags in the dykes are bleached & brown
Docks by its sides are dry & dead
All but the ivy bows are brown
Upon each leaning dotterels head

Crimsoned with awes the awthorns bend
Oer meadow dykes & rising floods
The wild geese seek the reedy fen
& dark the storm comes oer the woods
The crowds of lapwings load the air
With buzes of a thousand wings
There flocks of starnels too repair
When morning oer the valley springs

Poetry written
while an inmate of the Northampton
General Lunatic Asylum

Graves of Infants

Infants' graves are steps of angels where
Earth's brightest gems of innocence repose;
God is their parent, they need no tear,
He takes them to his bosom from earth's woes,
A bud their life-time and a flower their close.
Their spirits are an iris of the skies,
Needing no prayers—a sunset's happy close.
Gone are the bright rays of their soft blue eyes;
Dews on flowers mourn them, and the gale that sighs.

Their lives were nothing but a sunny shower,
Melting on flowers as tears melt from the eye:
Their death were dew-drops on heaven's amaranthine bower,
'Twas told on flowers as summer gales went by.
They bowed and trembled yet they left no sigh
And the sun smiled to show their end was well.
Infants have nought to weep for ere they die.
All prayers are needless—beads they need not tell;
White flowers their mourners are, nature their passing bell.

Stanzas

Black absence hides upon the past—
    I quite forget thy face
And memory like the angry blast
    Will love's last smile erase.
I try to think of what has been
    But all is blank to me
And other faces pass between
    My early love and thee.

I try to trace thy memory now
    And only find thy name;
Those inky lashes on thy brow,
    Black hair and eyes the same;
Thy round pale face of snowy dyes,
    There's nothing paints thee there;
A darkness comes before my eyes
    For nothing seems so fair.

I knew thy name so sweet and young,
    'Twas music to my ears,
A silent word upon my tongue,
    A hidden thought for years.
Dark hair and lashes swarthy too
    Arched on thy forehead pale—
All else is vanished from my view
    Like voices on the gale.

To Mary

I sleep with thee and wake with thee
And yet thou art not there;
I fill my arms with thoughts of thee
And press the common air.
Thy eyes are gazing upon mine
When thou art out of sight;
My lips are always touching thine
At morning, noon and night.

I think and speak of other things
To keep my mind at rest;
But still to thee my memory clings
Like love in woman's breast.
I hide it from the world's wide eye
And think and speak contrary;
But soft the wind comes from the sky
And whispers tales of Mary.

The night wind whispers in my ear,
The moon shines in my face;
A burden still of chilling fear
I find in every place.
The breeze is whispering in the bush
And the dew-fall from the tree,
All sighing on and will not hush
Some pleasant tales of thee.

A Vision

I lost the love of heaven above,
I spurned the lust of earth below,
I felt the sweets of fancied love
And hell itself my only foe.

I lost earth's joys but felt the glow
Of heaven's flame abound in me
Till loveliness and I did grow
The bard of immortality.

I loved but woman fell away
I hid me from her faded fame,
I snatched the sun's eternal ray
And wrote till earth was but a name.

In every language upon earth,
On every shore, o'er every sea,
I gave my name immortal birth
And kept my spirit with the free.

Sonnet

Poets love nature and themselves are love,
The scorn of fools and mock of idle pride.
The vile in nature worthless deeds approve,
They court the vile and spurn all good beside.
Poets love nature like the calm of heaven,
Her gifts like heaven's love spread far and wide,
In all her works there are no signs of leaven,
Sorrow abashes from her simple pride,
Her flowers like pleasures have their season's birth
And bloom through region here below,
They are her very scriptures upon earth
And teach us simple mirth where'er we go.
Even in prison they can solace me
For where they bloom God is, and I am free.

An Invite to Eternity

Say, wilt thou go with me, sweet maid,
Say, maiden, wilt thou go with me
Through the valley-depths of shade,
Of night and dark obscurity,
Where the path hath lost its way,
Where the sun forgets the day,
Where there's nor light nor life to see,
Sweet maiden, wilt thou go with me?

Where stones will turn to flooding streams,
Where plains will rise like oceaned waves,
Where life will fade like visioned dreams
And mountains darken into caves,
Say, maiden, wilt thou go with me
Through this sad non-identity,
Where parents live and are forgot
And sisters live and know us not?

Say, maiden, wilt thou go with me
In this strange death of life to be,
To live in death and be the same,
Without this life or home or name,
At once to be and not to be,
That was and is not—yet to see

Things pass like shadows, and the sky
Above, below, around us lie?

The land of shadows wilt thou trace
And look—nor know each other's face,
The present mixed with reason gone,
And past and present all as one?
Say, maiden, can thy life be led
To join the living with the dead?
Then trace thy footsteps on with me:
We are wed to one eternity.

The Dying Child

He could not die when trees were green
    For he loved the time too well;
His little hands when flowers were seen
    Was held for the blue-bell
        As he was carried o'er the green.

His eye glanced at the white-nosed bee,
    He knew those children of the spring:
When he was well and on the lea
    He held one in his hand to sing,
        Which filled his little heart with glee.

Infants, the children of the spring,
    How can an infant die
When butterflies are on the wing,
    Green grass and such a sky?
        How can an infant die at spring?

He held his hand for daisies white
    And then for violets blue,
And took them all to bed at night
    What in the green fields grew,
        As childhood's sweet delight.

And then he shut his little eyes
　　And flowers would notice not;
Birds' nests and eggs made no surprise
　　Nor any blossoms got:
　　　　All met with plaintive sighs.

When winter came and blasts did sigh
　　And bare was plain and tree,
As he for ease in bed did lie
　　His soul seemed with the free,
　　　　He died so quietly.

The Invitation

Let us go in the fields, love, and see the green tree;
Let's go in the meadows and hear the wild bee;
There's plenty of pleasure for you, love, and me
    In the mirth and the music of nature.
We can stand in the path, love, and hear the birds sing
And see the wood pigeon snap loud on the wing,
While you stand beside me, a beautiful thing,
    Health and beauty in every feature.

We can stand by the brig-foot and see the bright things
On the sun-shining water that merrily springs
Like sparkles of fire in their mazes and rings
    While the insects are glancing, and twitters
You see naught in shape but hear a deep song
That lasts through the sunshine the whole summer long,
That pierces the ear as the heat gathers strong,
    And the lake like a burning fire glitters.

We can stand in the field, love, and gaze o'er the corn,
See the lark from her wing shake the dews of the morn;
Through the dew-beaded woodbine the gale is just born
    And there we can wander, my dearie.
We can walk by the wood where the rabbits pop in,
Where the bushes are few and the hedge gapped and thin;

There's a wild-rosy bower and a place to rest in,
    So we can walk in and rest when we're weary.

The skylark, my love, from the barley is singing,
The hare from her seat of wet clover is springing,
The crow to its nest on the tall elm swinging
    Bears a mouthful of worms for its young.
We'll down the green meadow and up the lone glen
And down the woodside far away from all men,
And there we'll talk over our love-tales again
    Where last year the nightingale sung.

Lines: 'I Am'

I am—yet what I am, none cares or knows;
My friends forsake me like a memory lost:
I am the self-consumer of my woes—
They rise and vanish in oblivion's host
Like shadows in love-frenzied stifled throes—
And yet I am and live—like vapours tossed

Into the nothingness of scorn and noise,
Into the living sea of waking dreams
Where there is neither sense of life or joys
But the vast shipwreck of my life's esteems;
Even the dearest that I love the best
Are strange—nay, rather, stranger than the rest.

I long for scenes where man hath never trod,
A place where woman never smiled or wept,
There to abide with my Creator, God,
And sleep as I in childhood sweetly slept,
Untroubling and untroubled where I lie,
The grass below—above, the vaulted sky.

Sonnet: 'I Am'

I feel I am—I only know I am
And plod upon the earth as dull and void:
Earth's prison chilled my body with its dram
Of dullness and my soaring thoughts destroyed,
I fled to solitudes from passion's dream,
But strife pursued—I only know I am,
I was a being created in the race
Of men disdaining bounds of place and time—
A spirit that could travel o'er the space
Of earth and heaven like a thought sublime,
Tracing creation, like my maker, free—
A soul unshackled—like eternity,
Spurning earth's vain and soul-debasing thrall.
But now I only know I am—that's all.

Song

True love lives in absence,
Like angels we meet her
Dear as dreams of our childhood,
Ay, dearer and sweeter.

The words we remember
By absence unbroken
Are sweeter and dearer
Than when they were spoken.

There's a charm in the eye,
There's a smile on the face
Time, distance or trouble
Can never deface.

The pleasures of childhood
Were angels above
And the hopes of my manhood
All centred in love.

The scenes where we met,
Ay, the joys of our childhood,
There's nothing so sweet
As those fields of the wildwood

Where we met in the morning,
The noon and the gloaming
And stayed till the moon
High in heaven was roaming.

Friends meet and are happy,
So are hopes fixed above;
But there's nothing so dear
As first meetings of love.

My Early Home Was This

Here sparrows built upon the trees
    And stock-doves hide their nest,
The leaves were winnowed by the breeze
    Into a calmer rest,
The blackcap's song was very sweet
    That used the rose to kiss,
It made the paradise complete—
    My early home was this.

The redbreast from the sweet briar bush
    Dropped down to pick the worm,
On the horse chestnut sang the thrush
    O'er the home where I was born,
The dew-morn like a shower of pearls
    Fell o'er this 'bower of bliss'
And on the bench sat boys and girls—
    My early home was this.

The old house stooped just like a cave
    Thatched o'er with mosses green,
Winter around the walls would rave
    But all was calm within,
The trees they were as green again
    Where bees the flowers would kiss,
But flowers and trees seemed sweeter then—
    My early home was this.

The Winter's Spring

The winter comes, I walk alone,
    I want no birds to sing—
To those who keep their hearts their own,
    The winter is the spring—
No flowers to please, no bees to hum,
The coming spring's already come.

I never want the Christmas rose
    To come before its time;
The seasons each as God bestows
    Are simple and sublime.
I love to see the snowstorm hing:
'Tis but the winter garb of spring.

I never want the grass to bloom:
    The snowstorm's best in white.
I love to see the tempest come
    And love its piercing light.
The dazzled eyes that love to cling
O'er snow-white meadows sees the spring.

I love the snow, the crimpling snow
    That hangs on everything,
It covers everything below
    Like white dove's brooding wing,

A landscape to the aching sight,
A vast expanse of dazzling light.

It is the foliage of the woods
    That winters bring—the dress,
White Easter of the year in bud,
    That makes the winter spring.
The frost and snow his posies bring,
Nature's white spirits of the spring.

Sonnet: Wood Anemone

The wood anemone through dead oak leaves
And in the thickest woods now blooms anew,
And where the green briar and the bramble weaves
Thick clumps o' green, anemones thicker grew,
And weeping flowers in thousands pearled in dew
People the woods and brakes, hid hollows there,
White, yellow and purple-hued thc wide wood through.
What pretty drooping weeping flowers they are:
The clipt-frilled leaves, the slender stalk they bear
On which the drooping flower hangs weeping dew.
How beautiful through April time and May
The woods look, filled with wild anemone;
And every little spinney now looks gay
With flowers mid brushwood and the huge oak tree.

Sonnet: The Crow

How peaceable it seems for lonely men
To see a crow fly in the thin blue line
Over the woods and fields, o'er level fen:
It speaks of villages or cottage nigh
Behind the neighbouring woods. When March winds high
Tear off the branches of the huge old oak,
I love to see these chimney sweeps sail by
And hear them o'er the gnarlèd forest croak,
Then sosh askew from the hid woodman's stroke
That in the woods their daily labours ply.
I love the sooty crew nor would provoke
Its March day exercise of croaking joy;
I love to see it sailing to and fro
While fields and woods and waters spread below.

Pleasant Sounds

The rustling of leaves under the feet in woods and under hedges. The crumping of cat-ice and snow down wood rides, narrow lanes and every street causeways. Rustling through a wood, or rather rushing while the wind halloos in the oak tops like thunder. The rustles of birds' wings startled from their nests, or flying unseen into the bushes.

The whizzing of larger birds overhead in a wood, such as crows, puddocks, buzzards etc.

The trample of robust wood larks on the brown leaves, and the patter of squirrels on the green moss. The fall of an acorn on the ground, the pattering of nuts on the hazel branches ere they fall from ripeness. The flirt of the ground-lark's wing from the stubbles, how sweet such pictures on dewy mornings when the dew flashes from its brown feathers.

Clock-a-clay

In the cowslip's peeps I lie
Hidden from the buzzing fly
While green grass beneath me lies
Pearled wi' dew like fishes' eyes.
Here I lie, a clock-a-clay,
Waiting for the time o' day.

While grassy forests quake surprise
And the wild wind sobs and sighs,
My gold home rocks as like to fall
On its pillars green and tall;
When the pattering rain drives by
Clock-a-clay keeps warm and dry.

Day by day and night by night
All the week I hide from sight;
In the cowslip's peeps I lie,
In rain and dew still warm and dry;
Day and night and night and day
Red black-spotted clock-a-clay.

My home it shakes in wind and showers,
Pale green pillar topped wi' flowers,

Bending at the wild wind's breath
Till I touch the grass beneath.
Here still I live, lone clock-a-clay,
Watching for the time of day.

Childhood

O dear to us ever the scenes of our childhood,
The green spots we played in, the school where we met,
The heavy old desk where we thought of the wildwood,
Where we pored o'er the sums which the master had set.
I loved the old church-school both inside and outside,
I loved the dear ash trees and sycamore too,
The graves where the buttercups burning gold outvied
And the spire where pellitory dangled and grew,

The bees i' the wall that were flying about
The thistles, the henbane and mallows all day,
And crept in their holes when the sun had gone out
And the butterfly ceased on the blossoms to play.
O, dear is the round stone upon the green hill,
The pinfold hoof-printed with oxen—and bare,
The old princess-feather tree growing there still
And the swallows and martins wheeling round in the air

Where the chaff whipping outward lodges round the barn door
And the dunghill cock struts with his hens in the rear
And sings 'Cockadoodle' full twenty times o'er
And then claps his wings as he'd fly in the air;
And there's the old cross with its round-about steps
And the weathercock creaking quite round in the wind,

And there's the old hedge with its glossy red hips
Where the green-linnet's nest I have hurried to find—

To be in time for the school or before the bell rung;
There's the odd martin's nest o'er the shoemaker's door;
On the shoemaker's chimney the old swallows sung
That had built and sung there in the season before;
Then we went to seek pooties among the old furze
On the heaths, in the meadows beside the deep lake,
And returned with torn clothes all covered wi' burs,
And oh, what a row my fond mother would make!

Then to play boiling kettles just by the yard door,
Seeking out for short sticks and a bundle of straw;
Bits of pots stand for teacups after sweeping the floor
And the children are placed under school-mistress's awe;
There's one set for pussy, another for doll,
And for butter and bread they'll each nibble an 'awe,
And on a great stone as a table they loll,
The finest small tea-party ever you saw.

The stiles we rode upon 'all a cock-horse,'
The mile-a-minute swee
On creaking gates, the stools o' moss—
What happy seats had we!
There's nought can compare to the days of our childhood,
The mole-hills like sheep in a pen,
Where the clodhopper sings like the bird in the wildwood,
All forget us before we are men.

To be Placed at the Back
of his Portrait

Bard of the mossy cot
Known through all ages,
Leaving no line to blot
All through thy pages.
Bard of the fallow field
And the green meadow
Where the sweet birds build,
Nature thy widow.

Bard of the wild flowers,
Rain-washed and wind-shaken,
Dear to thee was mild showers
And heaths o' green bracken;
The song o' the wild bird
Than nothing seemed dearer,
The low o' the mild herd
And sheep bleating nearer.

Bard o' the sheep pen,
The stack yard and stable,
The hovel in bracken glen
Where a stone makes a table.
There the white daisy blooms

With a tear in his eye,
There Jenny Wren comes
When winter is by,

Comes there and builds anew
His pudding-bag nest
Hidden from rain and dew,
The milking cows' guest.
Bard o' the mossy shed,
Live on for ages:
Daisies bloom by thy bed
And live in thy pages.

The Yellowhammer

When shall I see the whitethorn leaves again,
And yellowhammers gath'ring the dry bents
By the dyke-side on stilly moor or fen,
Feathered wi' love and nature's good intents?
Rude is the nest this architect invents,
Rural the place, wi' cart-ruts by dyke-side;
Dead grass, horse hair and downy-headed bents
Tied to dead thistles she doth well provide,
Close to a hill o' ants where cowslips bloom
And shed o'er meadows far their sweet perfume.
In early spring when winds blow chilly cold
The yellowhammer trailing grass will come
To fix a place and choose an early home
With yellow breast and head of solid gold.

How Can I Forget

That farewell voice of love is never heard again,
Yet I remember it and think on it with pain:
I see the place she spoke when passing by,
The flowers were blooming as her form drew nigh,
That voice is gone, with every pleasing tone—
Loved but one moment and the next alone.
'Farewell' the winds repeated as she went
Walking in silence through the grassy bent;
The wild flowers—they ne'er looked so sweet before—
Bowed in farewells to her they'll see no more.
In this same spot the wild flowers bloom the same
In scent and hue and shape, ay, even name.
'Twas here she said farewell and no one yet
Has so sweet spoken—How can I forget?

To John Clare

Well, honest John, how fare you now at home?
The spring is come and birds are building nests,
The old cock robin to the sty is come
With olive feathers and its ruddy breast,
And the old cock with wattles and red comb
Struts with the hens and seems to like some best,
Then crows and looks about for little crumbs
Swept out by little folks an hour ago;
The pigs sleep in the sty, the book man comes,
The little boys lets home-close nesting go
And pockets tops and taws where daisies bloom
To look at the new number just laid down
With lots of pictures and good stories too
And Jack-the-giant-killer's high renown.

Birds' Nests

The very child might understand
The De'il had business on his hand
ROBERT BURNS

'Tis spring, warm glows the south,
Chaffinches carry the moss in his mouth
To the filbert hedges all day long
And charms the poet with his beautiful song
—The wind blows blea o'er the sedgy fen,
But warm the sun shines by the little wood
Where the old cow at her leisure chews her cud.

GLOSSARY
SOURCES
INDEX

GLOSSARY

'AWE hawthorn berry

BALKS strips of grass between ploughed fields

BEAVER fur hat

BEE-SPELL pattern of dots in marbles, resembling swarm of bees

BENTS coarse stems of grass

BESOMED swept (with a besom)

BLEA exposed

BRAKES ferns; more generally, thickets of bramble bushes

BRAWN boar; also male prostitute

BRIG bridge

BUMBARREL long-tailed tit

BURTON-HOLD Burton Wold, village in Northamptonshire

CAT GALLOWS STICKS two sticks stuck vertically in ground with third horizontally across them

CHILDERN children

CHOCK pitching marbles into a hole

CLACK chatter

CLINK AND BANDY game involving striking a piece of wood placed on the ground

CLOCK-A-CLAY ladybird

CLODHOPPER wheatear (small bird)

CLOSEN small enclosures or fields

CLOUTED patched

CLUMPSING numb with cold

CRABS crab apples

CRANKLE bend, wind

CRIM. CON. 'criminal conversation' (adulterous sex)

CRIMPED (also CRIMPLING) wrinkled

CRIZZLING crisp, just frozen over

CROSS-BUNS spicy buns marked with a cross

CROW-FLOWER buttercup

CROW-POT-STONE fossil shell, gryphite

CRUMPING the sound of snow as it is walked on

CUCK chuck, throw

CUCKOO-FLOWER early purple orchid

CURDLED curled, twisted

DICKEY back seat of a carriage (but also slang for penis)

DIMPS dimples

DIMUTE diminutive

DIPPLES dips

DITHERING shivering with cold

DIZEN dressed up in holiday finery

DOTTEREL pollard-tree (i.e., lopped to produce close rounded head of young branches)

DOWIE dreary

DRABBLED dirtied, splashed with mud

DUCK AND DRAKE game of skimming stones over water

DUCKING-STONE game involving throwing stones at a stone

DUSTMILLS channels drawn with a boy's finger

DYKE ditch or bank

FIRETAIL redstart (species of finch)
FLAGS rushes, reeds
FLAZE smoky flame
FLIRTING flitting
FLUSK fly with sudden and disordered motion
FRIT frightened
FRITTERED sprinkled
FUNNING cheating
FURMETY drink of baked wheat boiled in milk with sugar and plums, thickened with flour and eggs
GRIZZLE darken, lower
GRUBBLING digging, uprooting
HAYNISH awkward
HEADACHE poppy
HENBANE narcotic plant
HING hang
HORSE-BLOB marsh marigold
JINNY-BURNT-ARSE Jack-o'-lantern
LADYCOW ladybird
LATHY thin, slender
MAX gin
MIDGEON gnat, small fly
MILLER'S-THUMB bull-head (species of small fish)
MORT lot
MOULDYWARPS moles
NASH celebrated architect John Nash (1752–1835)
NINE-PEG-MORRIS game played on squares cut in turf
ODDLING solitary; odd-one-out
OLD-MAN'S-BEARD *Clematis vitalba* plant, also known as 'traveller's joy'
PEEP single blossom of flower that grows in a cluster
PELLITORY plant of the nettle family
PETTICHAP willow warbler (small bird)
PINGLE clump of trees, smaller than a spinney

PISMIRE ant
PLEACHY mellow, powdery
POOTY snail
PRINCESS FEATHER lilac
PROGGLING (*also* PROGGED) poking
PUDDOCK kite (small bird of prey)
RAMP grow luxuriantly
RAMPING *adjective*: coarse and large, applied to wild and luxuriant vegetation; *verb*: climb, scramble
RANK luxuriantly
ROLL roller for breaking clods of earth (horse-drawn)
ROUT a great stir or bustle
SAFFORN saffron (orange-yellow)
SALLOW a species of *Salix* (genus including willows)
SAWNS saunters
SCROWED lined
SEXPOOLS rainwater pools in areas where peat has been dug out
SHEEP-TRAY large hurdle
SHOCKS sheaves of corn, standing to dry
SLIVETH slips imperceptibly
SLUR slide
SNUB-OAK oak tree stump
SOCK moisture that collects in soil
SOODLES saunters lazily by
SOOTH true, genuine
SOSH plunge, dip in flight
SPINDLE shoot up (of vegetation)
SPRENT sprinkled
STARNEL starling
STIRTLING startled
STOVEN tree-stump
STULP tree-stump
STRUTTLE species of small fish
SUTHERING heavy sighing or whistling of the wind
SWAILY shady

SWATH row of scythed grass
SWEE swing
SWOOF grief, deep sigh
SWOPPING swooping
TAW marble
TEASEL plant with large prickly head
TOWN OF TROY puzzle involving
   a maze
TRAPS warders (in a madhouse)
TREPID agitated, trembling, fearful
TWITTERS sounds of birds twittering
UNBRUNT unharmed
WEDGWOOD celebrated manufacturer
   of ceramics
WHISP bundle of hay
WITCHENS wych-elms

SOURCES

NMS denotes manuscripts in the John Clare Collection in the Northampton Central Library (where they are catalogued by number), and PMS denotes manuscripts in the John Clare Collection in the Peterborough Museum and Art Gallery (where they are catalogued by letter and number).

Early Poems

'To the Fox Fern': PMS D2. 'Schoolboys in Winter': NMS 17. 'To an Infant Sister in Heaven': NMS 32 ('untained' in line 4, suggestive of both 'unstained' and 'untainted', was printed as 'untamed' when the poem was published in the *London Magazine*, August 1821). 'A Moment's Rapture While Bearing the Lovely Weight of A. S—r—s': NMS 1. 'A Ramble': NMS 7. 'Dedication to Mary': PMS A30 (variants from A29).

Poems, Descriptive of Rural Life and Scenery

From first edition (1820), checked against original manuscripts.

The Village Minstrel, and Other Poems

From first edition (2 vols., 1821), checked against original manuscripts. One censored phrase ('Jinny-burnt-arse') in 'The Village Minstrel', stanzas 5 and 6 of 'To an Infant Daughter' and some dialect words in 'The Last of March' restored from manuscript.

The Parish

'[Miss Peevish Scornful]' and 'The Progress of Cant': PMS A40. 'The Overseer': *Stamford Champion*, 5 January 1830, checked against original manuscript.

The Shepherd's Calendar

All poems except extracts from 'July' and 'October': from first edition (1827), corrected from original manuscripts, with some dialect words and original phrases restored (e.g., in 'January', 'dithering' for printed text's 'withering' and 'midgeon' for 'midge'; in 'May', 'sawns' for printed text's 'saunters'). Extracts from 'July' and 'October' are transcriptions from manuscripts: part of fair copy of 'July' (PMS A20), which was rejected by Clare's publisher (a new poem was written in its place); part of early draft of 'October' (PMS A18), including lines that were later developed into 'The Moors'.

'   The Moors': Carl H. Pforzheimer Library Collection, New York Public Library, manuscript 198. 'Travel' capitalised in line 54, since it is a personification (unless Clare meant to write 'traveller'—there are many slips of the pen in his manuscripts).

The Midsummer Cushion

'Shadows of Taste', 'Childhood', 'The Moorhen's Nest', 'The Progress of Rhyme', 'Remembrances', 'Swordy Well', 'Emmonsails Heath in Winter': Pforzheimer Library manuscript 196. 'Love and Memory', 'The Fallen Elm', 'The Landrail', 'Pastoral Poesy', 'The Wren', 'Wood Pictures in Spring', 'The Hollow Tree', 'The Sand Martin': PMS A54. 'Thee' and 'thy' addressed near the end of 'The Progress of Rhyme' in Pforzheimer text is 'Mary' in earlier (PMS A54) text.

The Rural Muse

From first edition (1835), corrected from original manuscript (Pforzheimer Library manuscript 196), with many original readings restored. 'To the Rural Muse': first nine of the poem's sixteen stanzas included to give the flavour of this 'invocational' poem that begins the collection; Clare himself revised this poem many times over, adding and cutting additional stanzas. 'On Leaving the Cottage of my Birth': a longer manuscript text entitled 'The Flitting' has nineteen further stanzas, but both the first draft and the published version end here.

Poems written at Northborough

'To the Snipe': Pforzheimer Library manuscript 196. '[The Lament of Swordy Well]', 'Snowstorm', 'Bumbarrel's Nest', 'Open Winter': PMS A59. Double sonnet on the Marten, sonnet sequence on Fox and Badger: PMS B9. Sonnets on Field-Mouse's Nest, Birds at Evening, Trespass: PMS A61. 'Glinton Spire': NMS 419.

Poems written at the High Beach Asylum

'A Walk in the Forest', 'London *versus* Epping Forest', 'The Gypsy Camp': *English Journal*, May 1841. *Two songs and some stanzas from* 'Child Harold': NMS 6. 'Don Juan: A Poem': NMS 6 (checked against draft in NMS 8; my text omits extra stanzas added into NMS 6 after return to Northborough), immediately followed in NMS 8 draft by letter to the unknown Eliza Phillips, which seems to serve as a dedicatory epistle and may thus be considered part of the poem's apparatus.

Poems and Prose written at Northborough, between two asylums

'Recollections of Journey from Essex' [*prose account*]: NMS 6 and NMS 8. Two songs for 'Child Harold': NMS 8. [*prose sketch*] ('Closes of greensward'): NMS 6. '[Lines written on St Martin's Day, 11 November 1841]: Bodleian Library manuscript Dc64.

Poetry written while an inmate of the Northampton General Lunatic Asylum

All from William Knight's transcripts (NMS 20, 2 vols.), except for 'An Invite to Eternity': *Bedford Times*, 29 January 1848, and the final two poems, 'To John Clare': PMS D24; 'Birds' Nests': PMS D27.

INDEX OF TITLES AND FIRST LINES